A Voyage of Determination

Anne Belovich

DEDICATION

To Barbara Cochran, the friend who first introduced me to sailboats and inspired me with her strong spirit of adventure and unique style of living.

CONTENTS

AN EARLY PASSION FOR THE SEA

I spent most of the early part of my life in Morro Bay, a small town located south of Monterey on the central coast of California. It is situated on elevated ground next to a large estuary that is partially closed off from the sea by a long, narrow peninsula. This jutting piece of land, crowned by a line of substantial sand dunes, was originally accessible only by boat since no roads reached the point where it joined the mainland. Across the channel from the peninsula where the bay merges with the sea you will find Morro Rock, a huge volcanic dome. This monument is part of a local series of nine volcanic domes that were formed in ancient geological times from the solidified lava of volcanoes, now extinct. If you drive from the nearby town of San Luis Obispo to Morro Bay you will see one of these domes next to the town and a string of them along the way in the form of abruptly rising hills that feature patches of oak woodlands alternating with patches of chaparral and large outcroppings of rock. Morro Rock is the most westerly of the series and because it was submerged in the sea in geological times past and is still exposed to waves and salt-laden winds it is more sparsely covered with soil and vegetation than the others.

At the time that I lived as a child with my family on its shores, the bay was filled with large, low-lying mud flats interrupted here and there by deeper channels of water. Most of these channels were filled with heavy growths of eel grass, but one of the larger ones was regularly dredged to furnish a clear, navigable outlet from the fishing boat pier and mooring basin along the peninsula and from there out to the open ocean. When I visited the town a few years ago I was saddened to find the mud flats and the eel grass beds near the town gone, dredged away to make room for more fishing boats and many pleasure craft, but less food and fewer habitats for birds, fish and other sea life. Somewhere I saw a sign that

A prisoner in the garden.

Anne and sister, Helen, digging clams.

proclaimed it to be one of the best-preserved estuaries on the coast. That didn't speak very well for the others.

As a very small child I was fascinated by the bay, where I could see herons stalking smelt in the shallow eel grass beds or I could watch the little crabs that made small cave-like holes in the hard mud that was exposed at low tide. Once in awhile a harbor seal would raise its head from the dark water. We lived half a block from the sandstone bank that rose up from shores of the bay. If I was allowed outside the house to play in the garden unsupervised for even a few minutes I would escape, run to the bank and race down one of the paths that dropped in a switch-back pattern between the heavy trunks of the eucalyptus trees that grew there. At the bottom there was a little beach next to the water where I could observe the wonderful things that lived there or hunt for treasures like old shells left by the Indians who ate the mud clams that lived here long ago. My adventures were always interrupted much too soon by an angry and fearful mother who imagined that I would fall in the water and drown or be eaten by a shark. Repeated punishments failed to keep me home. I was drawn to the water along with the seals and herons as though by some powerful instinct. I also seem to have been born with a spirit of adventure and a resolve to ignore danger.

As I got older and more emancipated I explored further and further along the shore. I learned to row a boat and was proud to be asked to row my grandfather out along the channel that cut across the bay so he could hold his fishing pole off the stern while he trolled for halibut. I was taken on family clam-digging outings on the north side of the Morro Rock where the surf crashed in on the sandy beach and where I learned about the open ocean that seemed to stretch out endlessly out from the shore. In the evening I would often stand on the bank near our house, where

Morro Rock in the sunset.

an opening in the trees would allow me to watch the sun go down beyond Morro Rock while lighting the sky with brilliant colors and then seemingly submerge into the sea. I would think about the vast ocean that continued beyond the rock and the exciting foreign lands that joined its shores. If I had a boat of my own I wouldn't be a captive of this simple little town. A boat would set me free to roam. When the colors had faded and the sky had begun to darken I would stop dreaming and would run home as fast as I could, hoping that dinner was ready.

I had an unusual outlook on life in general as I grew up and it came partly from my choice of reading. I learned to read early and especially enjoyed stories of adventure in exotic lands. There was very little other than reading to occupy me during the long evenings in our home. Of course, it was before television was even dreamed of and my father had a special ownership over the radio. He sat in front of it with his right hand just inches from the dial that controlled the choice of stations. It was nearly always tuned into sporting events like baseball games or boxing matches, which he called prize fights. The family bookcase contained a wonderful collection of English literature including an entire set of the works of Henry Rider Haggard, an English author of the late 19th century. He wrote both historical and adventure novels, many about Africa. I read them all, some several times. When I was 10 years old I could give a good account of the settlement of South Africa by the Dutch, discuss the life and death of Cleopatra and name the last three African Zulu kings. That whole amazing world lay beyond the sea. I felt that I was trapped by fate in the most ordinary existence in a small town located in a dull, modern, civilized country.

At school I found a book about the history of boats that included pictures of tall sailing ships. I was captured by the beauty of the ships under sail, but I wondered how people were able to climb those masts with the boat moving in every direction with the wind and waves. There was an old hotel in town that was home to some old men who had been sailors in their earlier lives on the kind of ships described in my readings. This derelict building stood on big pilings anchored into the sandstone bank leading down to the bay. The paint had worn off the warped siding long ago, patches of shingles were missing on the roof and other signs of wear offended the eyes of proper citizens. This included my mother who, inexplicably, called it the Bucket of Blood. If I met one of the old sailors on the street I would shyly say "hello!" Usually, the old fellow greeted me and went on by, but occasionally one of them would stop and sit down with me on one of the public benches placed along the street. I would ask him about sailing on the tall ships and then listen with fascination to his stories. One day when I came home from school my mother showed me a small, simple model ship that was made out of castoff materials like pieces of wood and wire and bits of cloth. She told me that a shabby old man with a long beard had knocked on the door and when she opened it he shoved the little ship in her hands saying, "This is for Annie," and ran off before she could say anything. I was sure it was a gift from one of the old sailors, a very special treasure. I added it to my romantic fantasies about the sea. More and more I imagined sailing someday beyond the big rock and into the open sea to follow the sun.

When I was in my early teens my father acquired a fishing boat. He was a civil engineer, but he was hoping to use commercial fishing to supplement his income from the few surveying jobs that came along in those depression-stricken years. I was very willingly taken aboard as crew. At first we fished for rockfish where there were rock formations under the sea beyond the big rock that stood on shore. We had a tin wash tub in which the fishing line was coiled so it could be let over the side of the boat without tangling. Numerous hooks were attached at intervals along the lower end of the line. They were baited and hooked over the edge of the tub as it was coiled.

After it was brought up with the catch and the fish were removed it was my job to untangle and ready the lines for the next casting. I became very skilled at this and all the rest of my life I have been adept at making order out of chaos with any kind of cordage. On our fishing trips, the job was all done during the pitching and rolling of the small fishing boat. Each trip was a small adventure at sea.

Anne hauling anchor on the fishing boat.

One day my father heard about plentiful schools of albacore tuna off the coast. They were being fished by trolling long lines near the surface of the sea with lures attached to their ends. There was a ready market for these fish at the canneries in Monterey and they brought a good price. A refrigerated barge from the fish cannery in Monterey was to be moored in San Simeon harbor where the company representatives would buy the fish. With the help of my grandfather, my father equipped the boat with folding outrigger poles, lines and fishing lures. They even made some of the lures from pieces of cow horns that my grandfather got at the slaughterhouse. Watching the operation and occasionally helping I was beyond excited since, as fishing crew, I would be going, too.

My father and I motored out of Morro Bay in our fishing boat a few weeks later at flood tide on a foggy summer morning, bound for San Simeon. It was about 30 miles from Morro Bay and would take about half a day by boat to reach. The trip was uneventful and tedious for a fourteen year old, but the late-day entry into the little harbor of San Simeon was unforgettable. Several hundred fishing boats from all along the coast were packed in there, swinging on their anchors to face the curving, narrow point that helped shelter them from the prevailing westerly winds. They were mostly traditional Monterey types with clipper bows and duck-tailed sterns. All were rigged with two tall eucalyptus poles that could be let down like slender wings to carry multiple albacore lines. Some of them had small rust-red sails that could be set for sailing back to the harbor with the late-day westerly winds like the Mediterranean fishing boats in their not-too-distant past. People were readying fishing gear and shouting back and forth. We could smell a fisherman's seafood stew called cioppino cooking. I was the only female in the fishing fleet except for an old Finnish woman whose husband kept her locked up on the boat because he thought she was crazy and was afraid she might try to kill someone.

We had an early dinner of canned Spam and boiled potatoes and were asleep by sundown. The sound of the slower boats getting an early start for the far-off fishing grounds woke us about 4 am. Some of them were powered by one-cylinder Hicks engines that the fishermen called one-lungers. As we had slept in our clothes, we were quickly underway. I took the helm while Father worked to get the lines ready for fishing. Out past the point, the air was still and the sea was glassy. Stars glittered brilliantly in a velvety black sky above the fishing fleet as the boats moved all together like a small town floating out to sea, each boat marked by its running lights. Toward the horizon, the lights of the stars and the boats merged and became confused.

Hearst Castle bathroom sink.

Looking back, in the midst of this magic, I could suddenly see the lights of Hearst Castle on the hill. Off limits to everyone except the Hearst family, the castle's powerful, wealthy owners, and their glamorous guests, it was rumored to be filled with marble and gold. A few years ago I visited the castle, now a state park, and observed that there really were gold bathroom fixtures, but they were gold plated, not solid gold.

The fishing trip was a financial success with a heavy catch of albacore. For me personally it was a life-changing experience. I gained a further love of the sea that would stay with me forever and would always draw me back. I would never live more than a few miles away from the sea except for some temporary arrangements during World War II. I knew I would find a way someday to sail away to distant shores and unforeseen adventures.

STOUT LITTLE SHIP

Narhval under sail.

Many years later after an early marriage, widowhood from World War II and remarriage my husband, Ralph Mower, and I found the boat of my dreams. She wasn't one of those glamorous greyhounds of the sea like the ones you see gliding out of a yacht club mooring basin. She was a 40-foot double-ended ketch; slow and stable with a broad beam, a modest Marconi-rigged

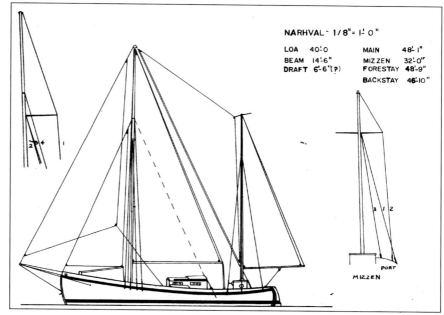

Narhval, basic sail plan.

sail plan and ultra sturdy construction. She had heavy double-sawn frames, was planked with two full inches of oak and had a heavy ballast keel, but no inside ballast. The origins of this little vessel were mostly unknown, but I was told that she was a North Sea pilot boat and was built in Göteborg, Sweden. I thought she might have originally been gaff-rigged. Boats of this type were sometimes called Colin Archers after the Norwegian-Scottish naval architect and ship builder who first designed and built them. Archer famously built the Fram in 1892, a heav-

ily constructed double-ended three-masted schooner used in both the Nansen and Amundsen polar expeditions. She was 128 feet long (39 m) and specially designed to pop

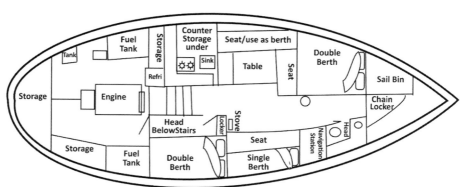

Narhval, below-decks view.

9

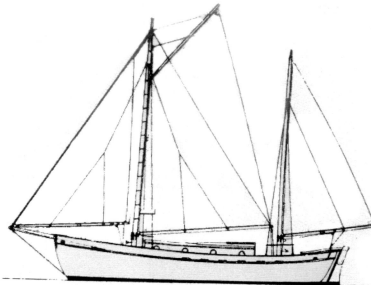

Tahiti ketch.

up and float on the ice rather than being crushed as was previously the case with arctic exploration vessels. The early, smaller Colin Archers were ketches or cutters, usually gaff rigged. They were used by a government organization, much like our Coast Guard, to rescue boats in distress and for patrolling with the fishing fleet where they could tow boats to safety in case of a storm. They were later sometimes fitted out as yachts. The first ones were built in Norway and later many were

Narhval, early photo in Europe.

built in Sweden. In the early 1920s an American boat designer named William Atkins designed some cruising yachts based on the Colin Archer concept. They became well known for their seaworthiness. Another boat with a Colin Archer legacy was the Tahiti Ketch, designed by John Hanna, an American, in the late 1920's. The design was so successful and so popular that hundreds of them were built. Some were gaff-rigged, as shown in the illustration, and some were Marconi-rigged.

Reading from the hull lines of the boat we had found, the date of building must have been in the early part of the 20th century. The story we were told was that Pingla, as she was called then, had been purchased in Göteborg, Sweden soon after World War II by some men who had just been discharged from the army. They took the boat to a boat yard in Hamburg, Germany, where they had the interior remodeled and dressed up to make it more livable and then sailed her across the Atlantic Ocean, through the Panama Canal and up the coast to Port Los Angeles. That was where we found her with many heavy layers of peeling paint, leaking decks, rusty rigging, almost unusable, weathered sails and a for sale sign. The bright side of this dismal picture was that her hull and masts were sound, she had an excellent Volvo

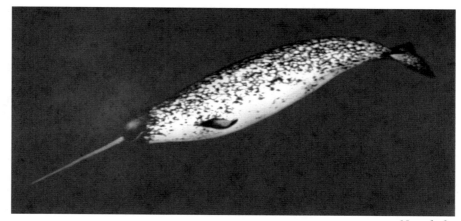

Narwhale.

diesel engine and she was exactly the type of boat we wanted at a price we could afford.

In a state of great excitement I purchased the boat with a small inheritance I had received from my grandfather and we renamed her Narhval after the arctic whale with a long tusk that I thought resembled a bowsprit on a sailing boat. The name of this small-toothed whale is usually given as narwhale, but I thought the old Scandinavian version, Narhval, would be more suitable since she was built in Scandinavia. The whale's spiraled tusk, which may have given rise to the unicorn legends, is derived from a canine tooth and occurs only in males. Since it is sensi-

Channel Islands, Anne.

Narhval at Lady's Cove, Channel Islands.

tive to substances in the water it may serve as a sensory organ. These whales are found mainly in the arctic region of the Atlantic Ocean. In medieval times the tusks were thought to have great mystical powers of healing. The Vikings killed the whales, collected the tusks and sold them in other parts of Europe for large sums of money. I had a silly idea for a short time that I would carve a spiral pattern into the bowsprit, but fortunately I abandoned it because of all the repair jobs facing us.

There was a great deal to be done in restoring our new treasure. Old paint was burned, scraped and sanded off and a gleaming new white coat with blue trim applied. The rusty rigging was replaced with stainless steel cable and new sails were made. I learned about a product called easy deck, a thick liquid that was applied to the deck along with a special fabric to produce a durable, waterproof surface. A sprinkle of coarse sand placed between the two final coats made it slip resistant. A number of alterations were made to the interior to make it livable. That done, we moved aboard with my teenage son, Rick. We lived on the boat at a dock in Los Angeles Harbor for many years and during that time we slipped away from the dock as often as possible to cruise around the beautiful Channel Islands that rose up from the Pacific Ocean half a day's sail away. Narhval was remarkably beautiful for a boat of such heavy dimensions and although we could never rush a weather passage she sailed really well and had remarkable stability.

Our lives also evolved in other ways. I returned to college to work on a graduate degree. I made new friends and cultivated new interests. Rick grew to manhood and went off to college. My marriage to Ralph Mower deteriorated, mostly because of my restlessness, and finally was dissolved. Since I had paid for the boat we agreed that I should keep it. Through our other settlements Ralph was able to buy a smaller boat of his own a short time later. We all went our separate ways except Narhval and I. She meant something to me that I could never fully understand. I was drawn by something stronger and more basic than a sense of ownership. So, she went with me, or I with her since she carried me and all my belongings as we sailed south from Los Angeles harbor to San Diego, a beautiful coastal city at the very southwest corner of the United States. I found a place to dock the boat at Kona Marina, a yacht facility not far from the downtown area and just across the channel from the yacht club. San Diego was the place of my birth and this was my first return in 40 years except for brief occasions of passing through. A return to one's birthplace should bring about a great change in one's life and so it did with me.

Max.

Nothing makes a middle-aged woman quite as attractive as being the sole owner of a 40-foot sailboat. Most of the offers weren't too interesting, though, and were probably directed more toward acquiring the boat than teaming up with me. Then the handsome, charming, slightly younger man named Max Belovich who lived aboard a leased sailboat down the dock asked me for a date. He took me to dinner at a restaurant a few blocks from the marina. We had a lovely evening, but when the time came to pay the check it turned out that he had forgotten his wallet and I had to pay for dinner. I really didn't mind and was somewhat amused at the time. I failed to take this as a warning

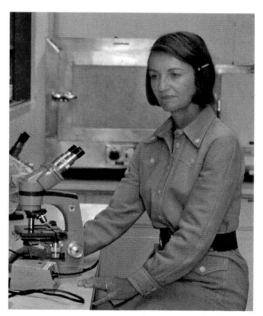

Anne, microbiologist.

Karl with Anne and Max.

from my guardian sea spirits and several months later we were married.

Soon after that Max told me that he would like to have his daughter by his former marriage come to live with us and maybe his son as well. A boat would not be a good place for a teenage girl to live so we would have to sell Narhval and move ashore. I was extremely unhappy with his proposal, but I was in love and couldn't find the will to refuse. We sold the boat to a man named Karl Putz, a land speculator and general wheeler and dealer from Cody, Wyoming who planned to sail it to New Zealand. He came up with a land deal for us in exchange for the boat and at first we wouldn't even listen to the "Old Pirate" as Max called him, rather unfairly. Boat sales were slow, however, and we wanted to get the matter over with and settled so we talked some more. We looked again at the land in Corona, California he was offering and thought it was worth at least as much as the boat. The sale was completed. We moved into a condominium near San Diego City College where I taught classes in microbiology and close to the county building where Max had a management level job at the assessor's office. I became a proper wife and stepmother with a great many personal rewards from my association with my new family, but I secretly mourned the loss of Narhval.

A trial sail with Karl and friends.

LOST AND FOUND AGAIN

Karl evidently had second thoughts about sailing to New Zealand because, after owning Narhval for a short time he sold it to Jerry Taylor, a friend of ours. Jerry found the boat difficult to maintain and sold it to a young local couple named Dee and Bob Roller. They enjoyed local cruising on the boat, but also found it to be more work than fun. After about a year of sanding, painting and occasional sailing they told Jerry Taylor that they were thinking about selling the boat. With perfect timing, Karl called Jerry and asked him if he thought the Rollers might be willing to sell the boat. So, once more he was the owner of the boat and with renewed interest in sailing to New Zealand. Karl hired Jerry Taylor, a skilled boat carpenter, to get the boat ready for the trip. Many good improvements were made, but a couple of unfortunate changes crept in. On Karl's orders Jerry replaced the open spaces below the bulwarks with some rather small scuppers. They looked better, but they allowed water to drain much more slowly from the deck than it had previously. Later, I found that if a big wave came aboard, the deck temporarily became a swimming pool and the stability of the boat was compromised. They also removed the big pre-filter for the engine fuel that often became a nuisance to clean. I guess it seemed superfluous since there was a small pre-filter and a regular filter with replaceable elements, but after the big pre-filter was removed there were persistent engine problems. The fuel tanks were the source of this difficulty because they were made of galvanized steel rather than a more suitable stainless steel. The galvanized layer corroded and sloughed little flakes off into the fuel as the boat rolled in the seaway. If the fuel wasn't filtered sufficiently the little rusty particles clogged the injectors in the diesel engine.

Karl was courageous, but the sailing trip to New Zealand was long and difficult and he didn't want to sail the boat back to San Diego. He put it up for sale,

Narhval is a killer.

left it in the care of a competent New Zealander named Bill Harford and thankfully returned home. I still remember the fateful evening when Jerry Taylor and his wife, Evie, came to our place for dinner and what should have been an ordinary, but pleasant social event turned into something more like an exploding bomb. "Narhval is for sale," said Jerry quietly between spoons of chocolate mousse. Max laughed. "Someone else can buy the fat old bitch! We don't want her." Then Jerry said, "Narwallow" and they both laughed. They went on like a pair of baggy-pants comedians with their matching mustaches and mops of curly hair. "Nobody owns Narhval. She owns you." "She's managed to find a series of servants who think they're her owners, but worked their butts off trying to keep her up." It was a very manly dialogue. "The poor devil that gets her will be fighting rust bleeders in the hull for the rest of his life. Better get it over with and paint her hull rust brown." "How about a mold-green interior to go with it?" I didn't laugh or say anything, but sat there with a strange kind of feeling welling up inside. Evie, who was sitting beside me, leaned over and said very quietly, "You want Narhval back, don't you, Anne?" "Yes." I whispered and, truly, I had never wanted anything so much in my life.

Someone changed the subject and nothing more was said about the boat. It was like a matter properly settled. Dishes were carried off and goodbyes were said. Max went to sleep almost immediately after getting into bed, but I lay awake for a long time. My pillow was too hard, then too soft, the blankets too warm, the room stuffy. I felt like I was choking for air so I got up and opened the French doors to the balcony. I went out and stood there in my pajamas. A breeze from the nearby sea swept into my face and I slipped into a fantasy that Narhval had sent me a message from New Zealand where she was moored and it had been carried to me by the winds of the Pacific.

I got chilled and got back into bed very quietly. Max didn't stir. I lay there and thought about our lives. We had so much to be grateful for. I was 49 years old, moderately attractive and married to a man who was so charming and handsome that any 20-year-old beauty in the city would have killed to be in my place. As an incurable romantic, I immensely enjoyed being in love with Max and I was amazed at his devotion to me. Together we had bought a lovely condominium apartment and two vintage Porsches, red for him and white for me. We weren't boatless, either. We had a beautiful 5.5 meter boat named Ringleader for sailing in the bay. But I still needed to be able to answer that call to the sea. I had lost my voice in this pleasant urban life. Narhval had provided me with a dream. She was a little ship that could take me anywhere in the world if I would dare to go with her. I wanted to get out of bed at that instant, put my hands on her helm and feel the salt spray in my face once more.

It's not very smart to allow yourself to follow desires that can't be satisfied. That's why I didn't say anything at dinner when the

Ringleader.

matter of Narhval's sale came up. I planned to put the matter aside once and for all. Max had a lot of respect for Narhval, but he liked classier boats with a good turn of speed. Something like Jerry Driscoll's black-hulled Sparkman Stevens ocean-racing sloop would suit him to a tee. He'd throw a fit if I suggested buying Narhval.

I fell asleep and dreamed I was sailing Narhval out in the middle of the ocean. There was an island just ahead and although we kept sailing toward it the island never got any closer. I kept adjusting sails and then adding sails including big square sails attached to yardarms that had mysteriously appeared on her modern rigging. The boat heeled down to a point of almost capsizing and I woke up suddenly. I decided to talk to Max. At least he would know how I felt even if he agreed to nothing.

I lay there with the clock and the dawn slowly advancing together. Max was sleeping on his back and when his eyes opened I was ready for him. I just blurted it out. I can't remember exactly what he said, but I remember his reaction quite clearly. He didn't look at me at first, but just kept staring with a shocked expression at his feet. He listened to my whole speech which was first of all a series of reasons for why we needed a larger boat and a second pitch for why Narhval was the best boat to serve our needs. He didn't say no outright, but he did point out what he thought were the weaknesses in my logic. However there was something in his voice that made me think he might be more than just a little bit interested in buying the boat that he had spent the evening bad-mouthing.

It was Sunday, a day of no obligations so we talked through the morning and clarified our positions. We loved Ringleader for day sailing, but we both wanted a larger boat with cruising capabilities. It had always been our intention since we were first married to spend our retirement years cruising the seven seas. We also missed the customary summer trips to Catalina Island and the nearby Channel Islands. Max had mixed feeling about Narhval. He liked the boat for its stability and safety at sea, but he also wanted to go fast. He had a way of piling on the largest sails we owned in defiance of the weather and would only take them down when threatened with disaster. His idea of the perfect cruise would be to put to sea in an ocean racer, have a spirited passage in the trade winds, put into a beautiful tropical harbor, stay in a good hotel and eat in exotic restaurants until time for the next spirited passage. During the time at sea the canned stew would be carefully paired with a French red wine and the tuna pasta would be matched with a good Chardonnay. I don't mean that he was a snob. He was just following his basic nature. He wanted life to be something other than ordinary.

I came into the boating world through commercial fishing and I feel out of place in yacht club circles. The adventurous trip by sea is what charges my dreams. Sailboats first appealed to me because they would allow me to travel over the sea for a long distance without having to refuel. Sailing could be fun in itself, but it could be a lot of work, too. I was drawn to the old-fashioned boats with big engines in addition to sails, spacious accommodations and stable hull designs. Narhval was basically my kind of boat. She had some faults, of course, but I was blinded like someone in love. Max was more clear-eyed. He had done little physical work before I knew him. When people asked where he got his well-developed muscles I would laugh and say it was from shaking the evening cocktails. Actually he drank Martinis which were stirred, but the idea was there. He was as strong as a horse from his good genetics, but had never developed stamina. The heavy maintenance on the boat ground him down and the slowness killed his spirit. After a long discussion he did finally agree to make the purchase, partly to have a cruising boat again and partly out of kind regard for me and my wishes. Once he committed himself to the action he proceeded with enthusiasm and determination with no turning back. Even though some bad times lay ahead he never expressed any regrets for his decision to support my romantic venture and never even hinted that I had foolishly led him on a hazardous course. He had real class.

Max came up with the idea that I would get a crew together, go to New Zealand and sail the boat as far as Hawaii where he would take over with his crew and sail her rest of the way during his summer vacation with a little extra time that he was sure he could arrange. I would have all of the three months during the regular college summer vacation period when I wasn't working for my part of the trip. I could easily sail to Hawaii with some time left over for stops at some of the South Pacific islands. I was pleased that Max would have that much confidence in me and ecstatic over the prospect of sailing across the South Pacific.

The sale transaction was completed. Carl agreed to partially reverse the original sale with us getting the boat and with him taking back the property plus $6,000 in cash to make up for some of the money he had spent on the boat to get her ready for the trip. We were able to raise the cash by selling Ringleader, our 5.5 meter boat which we would no longer need. Carl assured us that the boat would be ready to go and we would only need to buy fuel and ship's stores.

I joyously wrote to Bill Harford to make arrangements for him to continue to be Narhval's caretaker until I arrived. I immediately bought a sextant as though it were symbolic of the beginning of the adventure. I had to live within a slender budget and the only one I could find at the right price had an inspection certificate

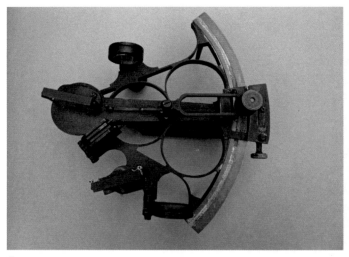

Sextant.

inside the box that was dated 1917. It was so old that it had a vernier sliding scale instead of a rotary scale, but it worked just fine once I learned to use it. Max and I took navigation lessons and bought charts of New Zealand, Tahiti, Hawaii and the South Pacific. I practiced my navigation skills by standing on a place above the sea on Point Loma, a San Diego suburb. This area is located on a hilly peninsula and is mostly surrounded by water. I was able to find a spot with a clear view of the horizon that would enable me to take sights with my sextant. Since I knew the latitude and longitude of the location already it gave me a good check on my accuracy when I worked out my sights on the local chart. I instantly knew if I was wrong if the results didn't show me to be at my known location on Point Loma. In spite of my urging, Max wasn't interested in joining me for such tedious activity. He was a man of action. Of course, his job of finding the continent of North America wouldn't be as hard as my need to find small groups of islands in the middle of the Pacific Ocean.

Anne in oilskins.

Then there were practical matters like protection from the wind and water while sailing. I ordered what was generally known among sailors as foul weather gear or oilskins. They were suits that resembled rain clothes, but were much heavier and covered the wearer much more completely so as to lock out the sea and wind. In those days they were usually yellow. I wanted the very best so ours came from the Helly Hansen Company in Norway, where they really know about life on the sea. A good pair of knee-

Gene Truex

Steve Gould

Harry Baldwin

Vince Herron

high boots with nonskid soles made for walking on wet, slippery decks completed our outfits.

Of course I talked about my plans with the other teachers at the college. My excitement over the coming adventure must have been catching because three of the teachers volunteered to go with me as crew to help bring the boat back. They were Harry Baldwin, a math teacher; Vince Herron, who taught mechanical drawing; and Gene Truex, a photography instructor. I knew Harry and thought very highly of him. I wasn't well acquainted with the other two. They operated out of a different building than the one where I taught and I had only had enough contact with them to know that they were good people to include in my venture. A young psychiatrist named Dr. Steve Gould, a friend of a friend, heard about the trip and asked if I would add him to the crew. We joked about it saying that if anyone went crazy on the trip Steve would really come in handy. Later on there were times when the stress was so great that I thought I might soon qualify. Several people from the assessor's office where Max worked said they would go with him on his part of the trip from Hawaii to San Diego.

We made more plans. Harry Baldwin took navigation lessons so he could back me up. At the same place where I bought the nautical charts I found a book called *Ocean Passages for the World*. It was published by the Hydrographer of the US Navy and gave detailed information on worldwide ocean passages for sailing ships as well as for power vessels with consideration for winds, currents and weather patterns. My book was a third edition published in 1973, but it was interesting to note that the first edition was published in 1895 when there were still commercial sailing ships. When you plan to sail on a long ocean passage it is very important to plan your route so that you can have fair winds most of the time. Pointing into the wind slows the boat down and a long course that requires constant tacking back and forth is really a slow way to go. Although a great circle route is the shortest distance between two points on the globe it may be a poor choice if the winds are against you. My new book showed wind and current patterns for the oceans of the world and recommended navigation courses to take between frequently visited ports. For my passage from New Zealand to Tahiti in the Society Islands it said to sail east with the westerly wind staying south of 40 degrees S latitude to about as far as 165 degrees W longitude, then turn north into the southeast trade winds and proceed directly to Tahiti. We could expect to cross a band of light and variable airs around the equator commonly known as the doldrums. It has been a major source of annoyance for sailors throughout the history of sailing. For the passage from Tahiti to Hawaii I also planned to stay somewhat to the east until we could turn toward our destination with the northeast trade winds on our beam or off the stern instead of heading into them and causing ourselves great difficulty.

I didn't own a camera at the time and wanted to buy one, but Max pointed out that I would have Gene Truex on the boat to take photographs. What could be better than having the college photography instructor record the trip? I agreed that I needed to watch expenses and let the matter go. Later on, when it was too late to reconsider, I realized that Gene and I saw things in a very different light. He wanted to show how difficult conditions were so he took many shots of wet clothes and bedding draped over the cabin and lifelines and photos of waves hitting the sides or stern of the boat. He and his friend, Steve, took pictures of each other steering the boat. They were shot while standing on the top steps of the companionway stairs so that the view showed the person's head against the sky. They were well composed and told part of our story, but I would have taken more photos of things like working the sails, cooking large meals in the small galley, reading the taffrail log or taking sextant readings of the sun and moon. Our photographs would have complemented each other to make a more complete visual account of the adventure. I was fortunate in being given Harry Baldwin's photos of some early important events and some from later parts of the voyage taken by Russ Morton, a young man who came aboard in Tahiti.

I wrote to Bill Harford and asked him to locate a dinghy, a small boat that could be carried on deck. He located one that he thought would be suitable and I sent him the money to buy it. It turned out to be made of fiberglass and the kind of boat you would ordinarily propel with an outboard motor, but it was probably more practical than the traditional rowboat I had envisioned.

Harry was on sabbatical leave so he was able to fly to New Zealand with his wife, Mary, a little before the rest of us were finished giving final exams. Mary flew home after a brief vacation. Vince, Gene, Steve and I flew down together. My memory is supplemented by a brief account of the trip in a notebook I had taken with me and planned to use for working out navigation problems. After much planning and numerous arrangements by mail with Bill Harford we found ourselves on the Air New Zealand plane headed for New Zealand via Hawaii. All at once I was very tired. I refused a cocktail offered by the stewardess which was unusual for me. I had been going full speed for several days and had suddenly come to a complete halt after getting on the plane. It was all up to the pilots of the plane now until we arrived in New Zealand. After we got settled, all sitting together in a center row, Gene got out a game, a kind of sophisticated puzzle, called "Who

Owns the Octopus?" We all set up our trays to hold the objects for the game, cardboard figures of houses, people and other objects. Vince read hints like "The Mexican smokes Kools. The Englishman lives in the red house. The zebra…." The men seemed to enjoy the challenges and the distractions from boredom that the game offered, but it was hard for me to get my mind off the adventure that lay ahead. I enjoyed the good dinner that was served and when tea was brought instead of coffee it seemed to mark the beginning of a new period in my life.

The night was terribly long. It was made even longer by the fact that the seats didn't recline enough for proper sleep. I felt almost as though I were sitting bolt upright. I'd doze off and then wake up with a cramp somewhere. This trial was interrupted by a stop in Hawaii for refueling. It was a beautiful airport, but it might as well have been in Patagonia for all we could see outside. People milled around buying duty-free goods and getting soft drinks.

Back on the airplane, we reset our watches to New Zealand time, two hours earlier. I thought about traveling with the sun, an experience in relativity. It was 1:30 am by the new time when we took off again on the 9-hour flight to Auckland. The crew soon passed around a small supper which I didn't really want. I ate a little and then set about going to sleep as best I could with people still moving around and chattering and a movie playing on a screen about 6 feet away. I woke up frequently, cramped and filled with anticipation for what the coming days would bring.

Finally, after what seemed like an endless trip we could look out the windows and see the shoreline of New Zealand—mountains, flat green plains and bays. We landed without incident at Auckland where we went through an

New Zealand, first view.

easy customs. When I was asked if I had any plant material in my baggage I declared my dried herbs and spices. I had to dig them out from the bottom of my sea bag. The customs official wanted to know if I was carrying a sail. I said "Yes and I'm also carrying a sextant and a compass." He seemed both amused and interested, but I was too tired to explain. We took a commuter plane to Whangarei, which put us much closer to Russell, our destination. Outside, the air was cold and the sweaters and jackets we had brought felt great. Being exhausted, we were really happy to find Harry Baldwin waiting for us with a little British station wagon. We collected our bags in the small airport building and had our first setback when we couldn't find out anything about our airfreight, even with several confusing phone calls. I had the impression that New Zealand phone systems were only for the most sophisticated.

Gene arriving in New Zealand.

We gave up temporarily, piled into the station wagon and soon we were riding on the left side of the road, through lovely rural lands covered with sheep-mown grass that was spotted with trees and shrubs. We wound this way and that way, crossed an ocean inlet on a ferry and came to the small town of Russell.

On the way to the boat.

Narhval was anchored out near the small Russell pier. She sat in the water like a huge white seabird, broad-beamed and seaworthy with a stern that tucked in like a duck's tail, without the feathers, of course. We went to the Harfords' place where we found no one at home, but we found some oars and went to the bay where the dinghy was pulled up

Russell, waterfront.

There she is, in the middle.

on the beach. We pushed it into the water and I got in with the crew and rowed out for a long-awaited reunion with my boat with my heart skipping a few beats. I know the others must have wondered why I insisted on doing the rowing. It was very special to have my boat back at last and I wanted to experience the whole thing. I actually would have liked to have been alone, but I needed to share the moment with my crew, who were eager to see the boat they would sail for such a great distance.

Narhval appeared to be my same dear old friend. I walked around, quietly touching things that were especially meaningful and silently thanking them for being there. The old bell from my father's fishing boat hung from the mizzen mast, the lovely binnacle that protected the compass still stood before the wheel. I found the taffrail log, the instrument that would give us the distance traveled through the water. The mounting plate was still fastened to the stern rail. When

Same old dear friend.

Compass.

Taffrail log.

Sample of cord from taffrail log.

we started the journey the instrument would be mounted there and the spinner would be attached to a cord of special construction that became very stiff when it was lowered into the water. As the spinner turned it turned the stiff cord which acted like a rod and turned the instrument mounted on the stern of the boat, which then displayed the number of nautical miles traveled. Those were the good things, but there also many signs of wear from Karl's trip. He had promised with great emphasis that the boat would be ready to go. I think he had good intentions, but it turned out that she might have been ready for some day sailing, but not a sea voyage of over 5000 nautical miles. Many things would malfunction or just come apart. This was something I probably should have predicted, since the boat had sailed in heavy rough weather for the same distance I would be going on my return voyage, but I only thought of my happy reunion. Harry complained about the bad housekeeping of Billy Frizzell, a young brother of Evie, Jerry Taylor's wife. He had sailed as a crew member to New Zealand with Karl Putz and had stayed on the boat for some time before our arrival. Harry had spent a whole day cleaning up after Billy and still didn't think the boat was ready for occupancy. I didn't think it was all that bad, maybe because my own house-keeping has always left much to be desired.

The boat was damp and there was no useable bedding aboard so we went to the bed and board place where Harry had been staying to spend the night in drier conditions. It was a little old house run by a rather worn-looking couple named Baker. They were gentle people with kind and loving hearts who were blessed with two bright and lively children. The children looked very young considering the appearance of the Bakers. One could have easily supposed them to be grandchildren. Our hosts made us coffee sweetened and piled high with whipped cream. I thought it was intended as a special treat for us, but later discovered that whipped cream was common in this fine dairy country.

A KIWI WELCOME

We were in town just getting out of the car to do some shopping when Harry said, "There's Bill Harford!" I easily spotted him from what I imagined he was like. He was dressed in overalls, a heavy sweater, wool knit cap and heavy shoes. He was tall, slim and strong-looking with a wiry build. He was talking to some-one and smiling a big, easy smile. I waited for a pause in the conversation and introduced myself. I don't remember what he said, but it was without artifice and his voice was warm and his gaze gentle and direct. He kept saying "Yis" with a kind of drawl that sounded to me halfway between British Isles and Southern United States. We were taken to meet Bill's wife Esme, who was working in her little shop. She was a stocky, handsome woman with a bright, winning smile.

We moved the boat from the mooring and tied up to the pier for a more convenient place to do the provisioning. The next few days were spent in putting stores aboard. I bought what bedding was needed—pillows and sheets, some blankets. We brought the old, damp bedding onto the deck to dry out. Plenty of water in plastic jugs was stowed away and enough food for four hungry men and one hungry woman to last for the long trip was pur-chased at the Russell village market. It included a quantity of po-tatoes, dry onions, cooking oil and canned meat, fish, vegetables and fruit. Bill kindly helped me obtain a plentiful supply of good New Zealand butter in tins. Some eggs were added, also jars of jam and some fresh fruit. Sugar, flour, raisins, chocolate, yeast and baking powder promised future homemade treats. Then there was kerosene for the cooking stove along with alcohol to

Bill Harford.

Narhval at the Russell Pier.

prime the burners before lighting the kerosene. Karl had left dishes and practical cookware including a couple of very large frying pans. Bill got some coal for the small cast iron heating stove in the main cabin. We were very grateful for it on the first part of the trip when it was wet and cold. Dr. Steve brought a doctor-type bag with first aid and basic medications. I wisely bought a hot water bottle for my bunk on cold nights. I'm sure I was the envy of my watch mate whenever I finished my night watch and went below to sleep in a toasty warm bunk. Even a wet bunk, and there were many, was better if it was warm.

I checked out the old sails and found them to be in pretty bad shape. Karl's wife had done her best to make some repairs, but all she had to work with was regular sewing thread that I knew would not hold up to heavy winds. It was fortunate that we had brought a new set of sails with us. The old ones would serve as a backup if there was an emergency. Little did I know how many emergencies there would be. We started the engine to check it out and had no problem. I still think of the unusual system for starting. First, all four cylinders were disengaged by moving some levers back. Now, the engine could be easily cranked with the battery-operated starter since there was no compression to slow the turning. As soon as good momentum was reached the levers were engaged one by one and the diesel firing in successive cylinders was initiated. If necessary, the engine could be cranked by hand using this method, but you would need someone with a very strong arm. After we had checked out the engine we made sure that the crankcase oil supply was renewed.

Doctor Steve and his meds.

We were ready to go, but a weather front moved in with strong winds from the east that would have headed us. I decided that it would be foolish to fight our way against them. We would have to wait for the prevalent westerly winds to return and push us along in the right direction. Bill and I glued ourselves to his radio listening to the weather broadcasts. Finally, on June 10 the wind swung around and we gave our venture the go ahead. Esme cooked us a delicious bon voyage dinner. I still remember a beautiful kiwi fruit Pavlova for dessert, a well-known New Zealand specialty.

I was strangely fearful that night about leaving on the trip. I had thought about the venture for a long time and all during the planning stages and the trip to New Zealand I

Filling the water jugs.

Drying out the bedding.

had experienced nothing but joy about getting my boat back until that night when cold, almost paralyzing fear set in. I wasn't worried about anything in particular. It was just an all-consuming, irrational state of panic. As soon as we left the dock the next day the negative thoughts disappeared and I relaxed and gave myself to the sea for whatever it had in store. Was it a premonition? Would it be like the old seaman's song from Australia about a woman sailor?

THE FEMALE RAMBLING SAILOR

Come all ye maidens far and near
And listen to my ditty
It was near Gravesend there lived a maid
She was both young and pretty

Her true love he was pressed away
And drowned in a foreign sea
Which caused the fair maid for to say
I'll be a female sailor
With jacket blue and trousers white
Just like a sailor neat and tight
The sea it was the heart's delight
Of the female rambling sailor

From stem to stern she'd freely go
She braved all dangers feared no foe
But soon you'll hear of the overthrow
Of the female rambling sailor

From stem to stern she freely went
Where times she had been many
Her hold it slipped and down she fell
And calmly bid this world farewell

When a lily-white breast in sight it came
It appeared to be a female frame
And Rebecca Young it was the name
Of the female rambling sailor

O come all ye maidens far and near
Come listen to my story
Her body's anchored in the deep
Let's hope her soul's in glory

May the willows wave around her grave
And around the laurels planted

May the roses sweet grow at the feet
Of the one that was undaunted

On the river Thames she was known well
Few sailors there could her excel
One tear let fall for the last farewell
Of the female rambling sailor

THE FIRST TRY

Official release.

June 11, 1974. The weather front had just passed and we were leaving the beautiful Bay of Islands under broken clouds and blue sky. We had just made an extra little trip further into the bay to Opua where we officially checked out with the New Zealand authorities. Bill had come with us to make sure everything went

Can't be true.

Broken mast and shredded sail.

Heading back.

right and Esme picked him up with the car and took him back to Russell. Now, everyone except Anne, who was at the helm, was gathered around Harry and the chart of the bay as we planned our route of departure. Spirits were good! People were assigned watches and began to get used to steering the boat and handling the sails. None of them had ever sailed before, but fortunately they were quick learners. The next morning, the **12th of June**, we were clear of the Bay of Islands and were sailing across the open ocean. We watched a beautiful sunrise, the sky filled with big orange and red cumulus clouds like enormous poppies floating over the sea. A swell was still running from the strong easterly wind that had kept us from starting our journey, but had now reversed directions and dropped in intensity. Gene felt fine. Vince was very seasick. The rest of us were mildly queasy.

A little fun.

A night of light winds and light rain followed. The morning was uneventful and I was feeling confident that the crew would be able to handle the boat and the journey would go well. Around 2 pm the wind picked up a little and suddenly, without any warning, the fitting that held the backstay at the top of the mainmast gave way and the backstay came down with a whipping motion. It didn't strike anyone, thank God, but the very top portion of the mainmast broke off, ripping the top of the sail badly. It was done in an instant! It was absolutely unreal. Was I was asleep and having a nightmare? No, I was having hallucinations. No, damn it, it had really happened. Our world had changed from one second to the next in such a minute flash of time that it was almost impossible to comprehend. We were happy and confident, sailing for the beautiful island of Tahiti and the next moment we were a group of bewildered and horrified sailors on a crippled boat. I could mend the sail, but there was no way to fix the mast while out at sea. We had no choice but to power back to Russell, about 130 nautical miles, and get the mast repaired. The option of giving up and going home entered my mind for several brief moments, but my inner sailor said no! I wasn't quitting! I assumed that the men felt the same way.

We powered all night, taking regular watches and pumping the bilges occasionally with nothing much else to break the monotony and absolutely nothing to lift our despondent spirits. The next day passed with light rain and a calm sea and from the cockpit where I stood I was tormented by a view of the broken mast and the torn sail bunched together and tied close to the base of the mast. Reality stared me square in the face with no escape. About 7:30 pm the rain had stopped and there was only a high overcast. We finally sighted the glow of the

Consultation.

Port Brett light. This light marked the tip of a long point of land with a jagged shoreline that went by the wonderful native Maori (Polynesian) name of Rakaumangamanga that I am sure I was unable to pronounce correctly. Many place names in New Zealand are of Maori origin, but no others have this elegance or complexity. About 1 am we passed Poor Knight's Island and changed course to pass to the right of Cape Brett where we planned to enter the bay and find shelter for the night. After powering for awhile I noticed that we seemed to be hardly moving relative to the shore. I checked the taffrail log reading and found that we were moving normally through the water. That could only mean that we were not making headway against the strong current coming out of the huge bay with the outgoing tide. I remembered a similar problem from when I crewed on my father's fishing boat. If we tried to enter Morro Bay when the tide was going out we couldn't make any progress. We didn't have a tide table that would give us information on how long we would have to wait for the tide to change. I told the crew I thought we should give up for now on Cape Brett and after Harry and I surveyed the detailed chart that showed the New Zealand shoreline I suggested that we go into nearby Whangaruru Bay, which was not so extensive and had a wider entry. I thought it would not have such a swift tidal current. We turned around, headed south a few miles, entered the bay with no problem and with much relief dropped anchor at the head of the bay.

June 16. We were all up at about 6 am to see the dawn with its delicate array of colors. The anchorage was very pretty with pastoral surroundings and sparse signs of habitation. Getting breakfast for the crew seemed to take forever, maybe because I was in a bad frame of mind from the accident and eager to get under way. I swore that it would be biscuits and tea from then on, but never had the heart to carry out my resolution. The bilge was quite full again. People took turns pumping the whale gusher pump, mounted in an awkward position next to the small doghouse cabin that opened into the main cabin. We weighed anchor at about 9:30 am after I knocked the cathead out of the way with a sledge hammer that I found in the engine room. I checked the fuel and found that the two tanks had not equilibrated. I had forgotten that there was a valve that could be closed or opened in the fuel line. I opened the valve and let gravity do its work. These procedures didn't even annoy me; they were so insignificant in nature compared with the disaster of yesterday that still faced me today.

We rounded Cape Brett about 1 pm and had no problem entering the bay with the incoming tide. We first went to Russell where we contacted Bill Harford. He seemed to understand the tragic nature of what had happened and was very sympathetic. He urged me to think of it as only a temporary setback and helped me to make arrangements by phone to have the mast repaired at a boatyard at nearby Opua. Harry and Vince decided that the trip to Tahiti wasn't something they wanted to do after our bad experience and informed me apologetically that they would like to return home. I was very sorry to lose them because they both would have been good sailors and Harry was my co-navigator, but I didn't blame them at all. I think that they had pictured Narhval as being more like a yacht instead of the old North Sea pilot boat that she was. She was uncomfortable and terribly wet inside and Vince had a problem with seasickness. The sea was heartless and the trip had an element of real danger. They weren't motivated by the same mad desire to get the boat back to San Diego as I was. I was actually surprised and very grateful that Gene and Steve decided to continue on. Still, a serious problem

Bill's son, Gerard.

remained. It would be very difficult to sail Narhval without a full crew. The sails were large and heavy and winches were small or nonexistent in some places where they were needed. We would not have a large enough crew to be able to have two people on a watch at the same time, which I thought was needed for sail handling and, most of all, for safety. It would put a lot of stress on Gene and Steve. I would have to take a night watch as well as cook and navigate which might take more energy than I had to give. Then, while I was worrying myself into fits over what seemed to be an insurmountable problem, a miracle occurred. Bill Harford and his son, Gerard offered to fill the empty spaces! If I had been able to carry a tune I would have sung hallelujah. Maybe I should have just gone ahead even off key and sung for joy. Bill explained he would be able to go only as far as Tahiti, but Gerard would plan to sail to Hawaii and then would fly to San Diego with me. Bill thought that Gerard might like to travel around once he got there so he could see something of the country. I should have questioned this part of the plan because I had observed that Gerard seemed to have some sort of mental handicap like mild autism or a brain trauma. In the front of my mind was the knowledge that he was a skilled sailor and that was what I desperately needed. It seemed that the devil, having taken me into great misfortune, relented and decided to back off and allow my adventure to go on. I would still be slightly shorthanded when we got to Tahiti, but I'd figure something out. I was becoming the most optimistic of risk-takers.

Bank at Russell.

With the problem of the crew settled, I called Max collect from a pay phone on the dock and told him what had happened. He acted like he could have predicted something like this would happen and demanded in his most manly, authoritarian voice that I abandon the boat and come home immediately. I refused and insisted that he send enough money for the mast and sail repairs and even had the audacity to ask him to have a spare mainsail made and sent to Tahiti where we could pick it up on arrival. I would have the old one patched up enough to get us that far. With quite a lot of yelling back and forth I got my way. Maybe I yelled the loudest. Also, people only have a limited supply of "no's" and he probably ran out before I did. The money was wired to the little bank that stood by the shore. From my end, I was determined that problems like broken gear and changes in the crew would not keep me from bringing Narh-

Opua pier.

val home. Later in the trip there were a few times when thoughts crept in to my mind that maybe I had lacked good judgment and should have gone home. However, any such ideas were always suppressed by an abso-lute iron-bound determination to carry out my plan.

We powered back to Opua, which was located on the curved shore of a pretty inlet further inside the Bay of Islands. Bill came with us to lend support. Where the curve formed a point there was a sturdy pier that we tied up to. People went into action with-out delay. I was amazed and truly grateful for their efficiency and industry. The boom was removed; the rigging detached at the base and the mast was pulled by a small crane mounted on a barge with the help of very skilled workmen. I began to put aside

Coming up to the pier, Opua.

Coffee break.

my feelings of shock and despondency and started to feel upbeat and optimistic, almost like it hadn't happened. This ability to quickly forget unfortunate and even dangerous events is probably what turns a person like me into a risk taker.

The mast was repaired with wood from the kauri pine *(Agathis australis)*, a New Zealand native conifer tree noted for its strong, straight-grained wood. These remarkable trees have the potential to grow to 150 to 160 feet tall and over 16 feet in diameter. The oldest and largest kauri pine, named Tane Mahuta, has a trunk of about 15 feet in diameter and 45.2 feet in circumference. They have cones like other conifers, but instead of the usual conifer needles these trees have narrow, flattened leaves. When the European settlers first arrived they found huge forests of kauri pines. By 1900 over 90 percent of the forest area was destroyed, mostly by heavy logging and fire. Conservation policies now help to protect the scattered remaining populations, mostly in the north where it is warmest. Many of our redwood forests were destroyed in much the same way before conservation groups made the heroic efforts needed to see that they were enclosed and protected within our park system before the old growth was all cut away. We are so fortunate to have people in this world with a passionate love of nature and an understanding of how fragile it is in the face of human greed. We never saw any of the large trees, but Gene photographed a small grove on an exposed headland that had been stunted by a stressful environment of winds and salt spray.

While we were waiting for repairs to be made, Bill's daughter drove me around to see something of local New Zealand and shared some things about its history that added to what I had been able to learn before I left home. I knew that there were two main islands, one to the north, where we were, and one to the south. They are close together, separated by Cook Strait which is only

Getting ready to pull mast.

Pulling the mast.

Working on the broken mast.

A small Kauri pine (Agathis australis).

14 miles wide at the narrowest point. Together they are about the size of Kansas. South Island is very mountainous. The highest peak, Mount Cook is over 12,000 feet. There are also a number of small islands (about 600), but only a few are inhabited. The native Maori name for the two main islands is Aotearoa which means "land of the long white cloud". It was first populated by humans in the latter part of the 13th century when the Polynesian people now known as Maoris arrived. The Dutch explorer Abel Tasman and his crew were the first Europeans to visit the islands in 1642. It was named Nova Zeelandia by Dutch map makers to commemorate the Dutch province of Zeeland. The name was later anglicized to New Zealand. Captain James Cook also explored the islands on several voyages beginning over a hundred years later in 1769.

In 1841 New Zealand became a colony of the British Empire. In 1907 it was declared a Dominion with a greater degree of self-government. Since World War II it has been entirely self-governing as the Realm of New Zealand with its own Parliament and Prime Minister. Today roughly 75 percent of the population is of European origin and about 15 percent is Maori. The remaining 10 percent is mainly Asian. The capital is Wellington and the largest city is Auckland. Narhval, my boat, was located in the Bay of Islands in the very northern part of North Island, north of Auckland.

The animal life of New Zealand is unique. Unlike Australia where marsupials evolved in the isolation of the remote sub-continent, the only original, native land-based mammals to exist in New Zealand were bats. All others have been introduced. Unfortunately this includes rodents, which are destructive to birds. Aquatic mammals like seals, whales and dolphins have always been plentiful in the waters around the

A view of the coast of North Island.

islands. A great many species of birds were seen by the early explorers. The lack of mammal predators allowed the evolution of flightless birds. Some, like the now extinct moa, were very large, as much as 12 feet tall, counting their long necks. By comparison, the African ostrich, the world's largest living bird, is 7 to 9 feet tall. The small flightless kiwi is a national symbol. New Zealanders are often referred to casually as Kiwis and may proudly call themselves by that name. People always refer to the kiwi as though it is a single entity, but there are actually five different species. They are all about the size of a chicken and all share some unique mammal-like qualities such as hair-like feathers, nostrils at the ends of their long beaks and bones with marrow instead of being hollow as with most birds. Their vision is poor, but their olfactory and auditory senses are well developed and their brains are large by the usual standards for birds. They hunt for worms and underground insects by sticking their beaks in the ground and locating them by smell. This is made possible by the nostrils at the end of the beak and

Brown Kiwi.

their excellent sense of smell. Extensive deforestation and the introduction of rats and other rodents by humans, starting with the arrival of the Polynesians about a thousand years ago, have contributed to the extinction of many of the original bird species, including most of the flightless birds. Dogs that are allowed to roam are a serious threat. There are now a number of preserves where the existing species of birds are protected and are making a comeback.

The kakapo, the world's only flightless parrot, and also the heaviest parrot in existence, is found only in New Zealand. It is nocturnal and lives to be almost 100 years old. The Maori people hunted them for their meat and colorful green feathers. The location of these unfortunate creatures is easily revealed by their strong, musky odor and has greatly contributed to their near extinction. In the 1970s there were only 18 male kakapos and no females known to be living. In 1977 some additional males and females were discovered. All presently existing birds, of which there are nearly 200, are closely protected on three islands that are free of predators.

Penguins have survived better than the other flightless birds, being marine based and unavailable to land-based animal predators. New Zealand, especially the smaller islands, and its surrounding waters are home to more penguin species than any other place in the world. I counted 14 species from a list of native birds. I always think of them as living in the cold waters of the Antarctic, but they range widely in the oceans of the Southern Hemisphere. The Galapagos penguin lives in the sea around the Galapagos Islands which straddle the equator. This is made possible by the fact that the waters there are cooled by the Humboldt Current that flows from the Antarctic. Penguins are able to spend about half of their lives in the sea because they can drink sea water without toxic effects. The salt is filtered out by special glands and expelled through their noses. Their little wings, which are useless for flight, are used as flippers for swimming. They are excellent swimmers and divers and the larger species are capable of diving to almost 2000 feet, although most of their food is taken near the surface. Their feet are set far back on their bodies. This helps with swimming and allows them to stand upright with the endearing humanoid appearance that we are so familiar with but makes walking on land difficult. I hoped that we might see some as we sailed away from New Zealand, but this didn't happen.

HOMEWARD BOUND

(Old Sea Chanty)

O fare you well, we're homeward bound;
Good-bye, fare you well, Good-bye, fare you well!
We're homeward bound for New York town,
Hurrah, my boys, we're homeward bound!

We're homeward bound, heave up and down,
Good-bye, fare you well, Good-bye, fare you well!
Oh, heave on the capstan and make it spin round.
Hurrah, my boys, we're homeward bound!

When the repair was completed the mast was stepped (installed) with a proper ceremony. Following a custom from medieval times, a New Zealand penny was placed so it would rest beneath the butt of the newly stepped mast. Then the rigging was put back in place and we were ready to go. I didn't know about the others, but there was great joy in my heart. We were homeward bound!

June 26. Ten days after returning to New Zealand we took the boat out and with Bill's help we swung the compass to calculate the corrections for deviation caused by various magnetic fields on the boat. These can be caused by any ferrous metal such as the engine, rigging, anchor and chain. Deviation varies from one boat to another so it must be calculated for each one separately. We would need these numbers to go accurately from compass (magnetic) readings to true directions or the reverse. I made up a set of deviation tables to use on the voyage.

Putting the rigging back.

Out to swing the compass.

Variation also had to be corrected for in navigation. This is the difference between where a magnetic compass points and true north for a given point on the earth. Variation is the same for all boats at the same point. I already had a table of corrections for variation on the boat I was able to use. I remembered the old mariner's ditty that reminds the navigator when to add and when to subtract. "East is least (subtract) and west is best (add) when going from compass to true."

We left the Opua dock at 6:15 pm headed for Russell. At about 10 pm we rounded Cape Brett and put out to sea bound for Tahiti. Since we were under power I had time to think what it meant to me to be starting out again. I was grateful to the people who had helped me and joyful to be given a second chance. My determination had actually been strengthened by my catastrophic experience. The thing that ran through my mind over and over was that I was going to sail all the way to Hawaii no matter what happened short of drowning. Nothing was going to stop me. Nothing! Of course, this would have been unrealistic if the mast had come down again, but I mentally refused to consider that possibility. For me the trip was partly a physical thing, but even more a journey of the mind.

The next morning, **June 27**, we turned off the engine and set the sails. The brisk wind continued to increase and suddenly the jib ripped and was taken down for repairs. The wind was pretty strong and things were beginning to slam around so we hove to under reefed main, mizzen and stay sail. Later we lowered the stay sail and put the wheel hard to lee. This calmed the motion and made us feel that the boat was under better control, but it wasn't what I would have considered an auspicious beginning for our grand voyage. I would have much rather had the sailor's dream of a fair wind, calm seas, deep blue sea and sky to match with big cumulus clouds sailing across it. Well, at least we were moving in the right direction and it was calm enough that I was able to sit on the cabin sole (floor) and mend the jib with my sailmaker's kit. The kit included heavy cotton thread, sturdy needles and a sailmaker's palm. The palm was a broad leather circular strap that fitted over the user's hand with a hole for the thumb. In the middle of the palm there was a piece of metal shaped like a little crater. The inside of the crater was filled with small indentations that would hold the needle in place while it was being pushed through the heavy fabric of the sail with the force of the user's arm. In the early days entire sails were put together this way. Now, it seemed like enough of a job just to make repairs.

A little later we took the mizzen down and the wind and rain stopped suddenly, as if by magic. In a couple of hours it was up again with a fury.

A helping hand.

Deviation tables.

Homeward bound.

In fact, it was so strong that we couldn't get the main up or all the way down. I have a note in the log that we lay ahull all night.

In the morning, on **June 28**, the wind switched directions to south-southeast and dropped its speed enough to allow us to set sail. We were blessed with a good wind, a glittering sea and waves that seemed almost harmless the rest of the day and night. When you go to sea in a sailboat you are literally ruled by the wind. You have to be prepared to live through sudden changes, both good and bad. Now we relaxed and tried to forget the strong winds and waves by watching the seabirds and hoping to see whales. A bird that looked like a big grey-brown gull flew by the boat. Fortunately, it didn't fly directly over us. It was chasing a smaller bird that suddenly disgorged its food. The big bird caught nearly all of it in mid-air and swallowed it with amazing speed and agility. I was pretty sure we had just watched a type of feeding known to scientists as klepto-parasitism, but to

Bill taking down the jib for repair.

the rest of us as just plain thievery. The large bird was a skua, a notably aggressive pelagic bird that lives mainly by stealing food from other birds or even killing them. After returning home I went to the library and looked up more information. The bird we saw was probably the brown skua (Stercorarius antarcticus), also known as the subantarctic skua or by the Maori name, hakoakoa. It is known to breed on the south end of New Zealand's South Island and on some of the smaller islands of New Zealand like Stewart and Auckland. During the winter non-breeding season the brown skuas occur in the open ocean off New Zealand and

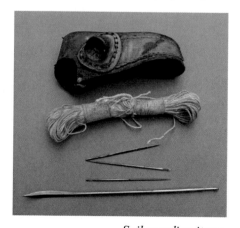

Sail mending items.

Skua.

other parts of the South Pacific. In their southern breeding grounds they often locate their nesting sites near a penguin colony so they can live partly by stealing eggs and chicks. The female skua usually lays two eggs that are tended by both male and female. The first to hatch is the largest. When the other chick hatches, the first sibling pushes the new chick out of the nest where it is left to die or it kills the other chick outright. It seems that the aggressive behavior is there from birth. These are all true facts about the skuas. One account that I heard somewhere long ago that may or may not be true is that the skuas would follow the old sailing ships and eat the refuse. If a sailor fell overboard the skuas would peck out his eyes. This terrible vision has always haunted me. Maybe that is partly what caused my obsession with not wanting anyone to fall overboard. I was an absolute tyrant about the crew wearing safety harnesses when they were on deck.

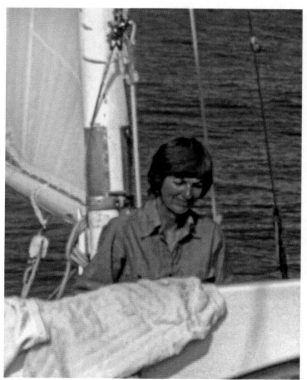

Anne on watch.

On the morning of **June 29** I took the helm until close to noon, happy because we were headed in a reasonable direction. Then the wind began to build up and the boat heeled down hard. She put her upper rail under a couple of times and I cursed the fact the bulwarks were sealed up. The tiny scuppers that were installed in their place were pathetically inadequate. Bill came up on deck and said that things were getting pretty wild below and suggested we drop the main. "We're in for a bit of a blow" he said calmly which translated into normal hysterical language meant "Jesus Christ! We're going to be knocked on our asses!" New Zealanders like Bill live so close to the ocean both physically and in spirit that they seem to have a sixth sense about what it will do. I quickly agreed to all prudent actions. He called for Gerard and together they doused the big sail and soothed Narhval's spirit, at least temporarily. I stayed on the helm and hummed the old sea chanty "Blow the Wind Westerly" about various sea creatures jumping onto the ship. It goes:

> *Up jumps a crab with his crooked legs*
> *Saying "you play the cribbage and I'll stick the pegs"*
> *Singing blow the wind westerly, let the wind blow*
> *By a gentle nor'wester how steady she goes*
>
> *Up jumps a herring, the king of the sea*
> *He jumps up on deck saying "helms a-lee!"*
> *Singing blow the wind westerly, let the wind blow*
> *By a gentle nor'wester how steady she goes*
>
> *Up jumps a shark with his big row of teeth*
> *He jumped up between the decks and shook out the reefs*
> *Singing blow the wind westerly, let the wind blow*
> *By a gentle nor'wester how steady she goes*

I could hardly believe how quickly the seas built up along with the wind. They peaked up higher and higher and then the tops began to blow away. There was nothing we could do but hang on and run. And so we did all day and night. Narhval handled herself like a lady, but now and then one of the breaking grey backs would pile onto her decks, filling them to the top of the bulwarks. Once when I was alone on watch, one broke with a thundering crash over my head and filled the decks.

Steve and Gerard.

Another big one on the starboard bow.

Bilge pump.

The water drained out the small scuppers slowly and I imagined that the boat acquired a dangerous, wallowing motion. It scared me more than it should have because it did no harm, other than getting me good and wet, and didn't happen again. I decided not to share my feelings of alarm with my crew for fear of undermining their confidence. When I was relieved of my watch and went below it was with a phony air of cheerfulness. I was learning some things from Bill. Smile and say loudly, "She'll be all right, mate!" Everyone would take the event in stride.

Water seemed to find its way into the boat in a thousand places. Furthermore, the stern bearing was leaking badly and the whale pump was out of commission for awhile. The rolling of the boat was dampened somewhat by the pressure of the sail, but we were under shortened sail, which wasn't enough to make it comfortable. Bilge water slopped up the whole side of the boat with each roll. Not only did she roll, but as waves passed under the boat she pitched fore and aft. Down below it was chaotic with gear thrown everywhere and water and oil all over the cabin soles. If the crew members who tried to find shelter below hadn't hung on to something they would have been thrown around, too. I thought of the old sailor's curse for the ship:

> *Pitch and roll*
> *God damn your soul!*
> *Roll and pitch*
> *You son of a bitch!*

Wave astern and albatross.

That night Bill and I stood the midnight-to-4 watch. As the moon came out from the grey-black clouds to light the 20- to 25-footers boiling up astern I talked about my lovely house in San Diego with its central heating and soft carpets and my beautiful queen-sized bed. It was a vision from another world, quiet, warm, dry and, most of all, immobile. I also thought to myself, in my own private world, about my husband whose loving arms waited in that bed while mine struggled with the wheel to keep Narhval's stern to the roaring wind. I wasn't feeling sorry for myself. I was just reviewing, with a kind of amazement, a picture from a world that was as different as possible from the one I temporarily existed in and was one entirely of my own making.

The next day, **June 30**, we ran before the wind all day as it abated some and in the evening tried unsuccessfully to set a reefed mainsail. The main halyard was

Anne and Bill raising the mainsail.

hopelessly fouled from having whipped around in the wind. Bill wanted to go aloft, but I asked him not to. It seemed a dangerous act with the big swells and approaching dark. As a boat rolls in the sea the mast moves with ever greater speed and a longer arc as you go higher and higher. Pitching causes a heavy motion in the fore and aft direction and compounds the side to side motion of the roll. It becomes harder and harder to hold on as you climb. It must have been a deadly force at the tops of the masts in the days of the tall ships whose sailors climbed in order to furl the sails to the yardarms. They would have had very strong arms. For that reason, stories and songs about women disguised as men who signed on as sailors were probably only fantasies created by men who longed for the company of women. There was an old saying, "One hand for yourself and one for the ship" that spoke of the limits of the sailor's obligations with work aloft. They were officially allowed to hang on with one arm while they brought in the sail or made a line fast. I thought afterwards that Bill might have been secretly relieved to have me object because he really didn't want to take the risk, but thought it his manly duty to do so. He agreed to wait until morning and at that time the sea was calm enough for us to haul him up in a bosun's chair with the main topping lift. Although the job was still difficult as he had to struggle to keep himself from swinging free with the rolling of the boat, it was soon done without a mishap. The rest of the day and the following night were unusually pleasant, a strange contrast to what we had just been through. Narhval sailed along with a happier crew and a skipper who caught a few extra hours of sleep. Blessed sleep that heals all ills!

The next day was **July 1**, a new month. Gene followed my request to put a cleat on the mizzen mast so the main boom could be lifted up and the topping lift secured for reefing. He was a good crew member, always taking care of every task with good nature and efficiency. They all had their good qualities and special talents, but handiness wasn't always there. Steve had a great sense of humor and kept us laughing when we most needed it, but was serious about his work in helping to sail the boat. Bill had excellent leadership qualities and was skilled at directing and coordinating operations like sail changing. Both he and Gerard were really good sailors. I was grateful for all of them there to help sail my boat home.

Being a woman with an all-man crew had some potential problems in the realm of personal privacy. I was fortunate in having a private cabin with its own small enclosed head. There was also a head in the fo'c'sle that could be used by the crew. However, since it is such a simple matter for a man to open the fly of his trousers and aim into the ocean, they preferred this instead of getting someone to take their watch so they could go below. We had an arrangement that they would tell me they had an urgent need and I would just turn my back until they signaled it was done. The Kiwis would always say, "I have to shed a tear for Nelson," referring to Vice Admiral Horatio Nelson, an inspirational and much-admired leader as an officer in the Royal Navy of Great Britain during the Napoleonic wars and other conflicts. Sometimes they shortened it to, "I have to shed a tear."

The mainsail was set in the morning to a beautiful following wind. The waves were still big, but less powerful. Bill saw our first flying fish giving promise of mahi-mahi, a large predatory fish that would be swimming after them. Mahi-mahi means very strong in Hawaiian. I have also heard them called dorados and dolphins. Dorado comes

Mahi-mahi.

from a Spanish word meaning gilded or golden and refers to the brilliant colors of the fish. The name dolphin is a misnomer because a true dolphin is a mammal. Mahi-mahi are powerful swimmers with long bodies that are compressed along the sides and a single long fin that runs almost the full length of their bodies. Their heads are shaped in such a way as to give them a seemingly angry or fierce expression. Their colors are amazing—bright iridescent blue and green. When caught and brought on deck the colors sadly fade as they die, finally becoming a sort of grey. I had seen this happen long ago on my father's fishing boat. A warm current of water off the central California coast must have brought the mahi-mahi north of their usual range because we caught one on one of our albacore trolling lines. We didn't know what it was and when it went through its spectacular color change my father loudly pronounced it to be poisonous. He wanted to throw it back in the sea, but I convinced him to keep it with the rest of the fish so it would be identified when the catch was sold. The fish merchant called it a dolphin and paid a good price for it.

Soon after, Gerard spotted what appeared to be part of a life raft turned over. It gave us all a strange feeling. We hove to for awhile and looked over the sea carefully, but could see nothing more so we sailed on. It stayed on my mind the rest of the day with a sort of fear that someone out there might need help.

The day passed peacefully with a steady wind. We watched as albatrosses sailed by. One was larger and different from the rest—grey with nearly a 10-foot wingspan. The old sailors had interesting beliefs about albatrosses. They thought it was good luck to have one follow the ship. There was also a belief that they were the spirits of dead sailors and harming them would bring bad luck. The strangest is the expression "having an albatross around your neck" meaning you are suffering guilt for an action that has brought misfortune to others. It comes from The Rime of the Ancient Mariner by Samuel Taylor Coleridge in which an albatross that is following the ship and eating scraps of food thrown to him brings the ship fair winds. The mariner (navigator) of the ship inexplicably shoots the albatross and brings terrible misfortunes upon them. The dead bird is hung from the mariner's neck by the sailors as retribution.

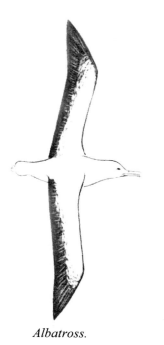

Albatross.

All in a hot and copper sky,
The bloody Sun, at noon,
Right up above the mast did stand,
No bigger than the Moon.

Day after day, day after day,
We stuck, nor breath nor motion;
As idle as a painted ship
Upon a painted ocean.

Water, water, everywhere,
And all the boards did shrink;
Water, water, everywhere,
Nor any drop to drink.

"Ah! well a-day! what evil looks
Had I from old and young!
Instead of the cross, the Albatross
About my neck was hung.

Biologically, the albatrosses are very large seabirds related to the petrels. They live in the circumpolar Southern Ocean and the North Pacific, but not in the North Atlantic. They may have a wingspan of up to almost 12 feet and are skilled at soaring by catching the rising air on the windward side of waves or by flying up into the wind and then down and forward with the wind. This allows them to travel long distances with little effort. They nest on isolated islands and form pair bonds that last for a lifetime, which is often lengthy.

It was **July 2**, another peaceful day with falling wind. Steve, who had been struggling with the miserable conditions, cleaned up and cheered up. The others took a more lighthearted attitude as well. Sailing could be a good life after all. I tried my first celestial navigation in

Anne navigating.

the morning. We couldn't get the time tick on the portable radio so we tried to use Gene's watch. I don't think it worked very well because my fix seemed quite unreasonable. I tried another later in the evening after the time tick came in. I took shots of both the sun and moon. It was better, but still seemed too far south. I planned to try shots of Venus and the sun in the morning so I could correct any mistakes I might have made. My explanation at the time was that we had made more leeway than I had figured on. We had had some fairly strong northwest winds that could have pushed us to the south. Additional sights over the next few

Steve the serious sailor.

days seemed to confirm this assessment. It also made me realize how much trouble a sailor could get into by relying on deduced reckoning alone.

Cooking, which was my job along with navigation and an occasional turn at the wheel, was a real pain in the butt! It took at least three times the time and four times the effort that it did at home. It was almost impossible to find ingredients where they were jammed into the crowded shelves of the small galley. While I was cooking, things had to be placed so they wouldn't bounce over the rail and fall off the counter. I had to balance myself or even hang onto something while I worked. Pots needed to be secured to the little stove by the adjustable rail. Yet people seemed to enjoy the results. It is said that an army travels on its stomach. I think a ship's crew does, too. With conditions often almost unbearable the comfort of food is very important. Since I was cooking for four men who were doing heavy labor, quantity was important. Karl left an over-sized frying pan on the boat with a lid that fit. I filled it with fried onions and potatoes and plopped eggs on top for breakfast. It was easily converted to canned beef hash for dinner by substituting a can of corned beef for the eggs. Hot oatmeal was consumed like it was the food of the gods. Fresh bread, hot from the oven, was on the schedule every other day with extra loaves set aside for alternate days. It went over in a big way! This night's dinner (tea for the Kiwis) was a big hit, too. It would be one of the favorites, creamed salmon and peas on rice and marinated bean and tomato salad. The beans and tomatoes both came from cans, but no one seemed to notice. Freshly baked cookies were always welcome. Narhval moved on wind and diesel, the men ran on food and I needed food as well, but my communion with the spirit of the sea nourished me and had much to do with keeping me going.

Everyone's attitude improved with the wind, a beautiful northwesterly—20 to 25 knots by the end of the day and we were making a good 6 to 7 knots. The deep blue of the sea reflected the blue of the sky. We watched albatrosses soaring ahead of the face of the waves. Gerard was feeling more himself and he was making himself quite useful. He was very happy with Max's boots and foul weather gear top that I had brought along. He started wearing them constantly although he had refused to put them on at first. He was sweet-natured and willing to help, but lacked initiative. He was a follower, not a natural leader like his father. Both Bill and Gerard really loved to sail and today was a perfect day for it. Off watch, Bill sat in the bow and watched the bow wave with pure enjoyment. Then he looked back over the boat for a long time and finally took the wheel from me so I could go to the bow, too, and look back to see what a powerful hull Narhval had.

Love of sailing.

I had planned to teach Bill some navigation before the trip was over because he wanted to start a business delivering boats for people over long distances. I asked him to sit down on one of the small cabin side extensions with me so I could show him how to work out a sun sight I had just taken. After just a few sentences of explanation he pushed the chart aside, waved his hands with annoyance and got up with an expression of great frustration and went below. That was the end of the navigation lessons. Too bad! I was sorry. Maybe he could team up with someone who liked to fiddle with numbers. The day's run was 123 nautical miles.

A SAILOR'S HARD LIFE

July 3. What a bad night! We were running with a quartering sea under main and jib in a wind of about 20 to 25 knots. About midnight the wind picked up some and we were broached by a freak wave and rolled over far enough to put the jib in the water. I thought for a few minutes that we were going over all the way. The jib was torn badly by the force of the water and the batteries flew out of their boxes and fell with destructive force onto the metal floor plates of the engine room. The butcher knife that was lying on the galley sink counter flew through the open door of my little cabin and stuck in the side of the hull next to where I had just been sleeping. The bilge water rolled right into our bunks. Oh my God, what a terrible shock to be awakened from sleep by cold water pouring over your back! We kept calling to the people on watch to pump and they kept yelling back that they were. Somehow, maybe from exhaustion, I went back to sleep. At midnight I woke to hear Bill and Gene banging around with bilges and pumps. The whale pump had quit again. I got up and we went through a long hassle of trouble shooting in the mounting seas. Bill discovered some holes in the line and Steve taped them up in fine surgical fashion. We all went back to soaking bunks with our hearts still pounding from the shock and exertion. We would try vainly to sleep a little.

Later in the morning the wind mounted again suddenly and Bill called that he couldn't control the wheel. I confirmed his request to drop the main and mizzen which the crew did in a beautifully coordinated way with Bill shouting directions in his fine Kiwi voice. In spite of the heavy rolling of the boat I worked on a huge breakfast of potatoes, sausage, onions and eggs. Then, I took the wheel so that everyone could go below for breakfast. I was really hungry and called for someone to hand me a plate of food. It was handed up and as I took it the wind gusted and wooosht!! It blew the plate clean. Not a morsel left for a hungry sailor. Shit! I spat out a few more elaborate seaman-like curses and decided to wait for the others to finish breakfast before I filled my plate again so I was able to go below and eat it in safety. I shouted down a few friendly threats to the crew sitting below, in the warm cabin, happily shoveling down food that they had better leave a good portion for me or there would be trouble. They did and I was soon relieved from the wheel to go and fill my empty stomach. From then on it was known as the Fast Food incident. Everyone except the captain thought it was funny and made jokes about it. As I wrote this a little later I was sitting in the doghouse and I looked up now and then to watch big grey seas with breaking tops coming up astern. Our speed under only the stay sail and spare jib was about 5 knots. The day's run was 146 nautical miles.

Big grey seas.

The next day, **July 4**, seemed miraculously quiet and everyone got some much needed rest. The mainsail and the mizzen were hoisted in the morning. We brought our bedding out on deck and tried to dry it, but of little use. The humidity was high, the temperature was low and the salt gave up its water very reluctantly. I spent most of the day sewing the jib back together. It was ripped completely in half at the widest part—right next to the clew and a good 4 feet of the leach blown away. Gene and Bill cleaned up the mess in the engine room. One battery was completely destroyed with both terminals broken off. We would have no electric lights now except for our center compass light. We would have to make do with the flashlights (torches in Kiwi language) and our one kerosene lamp. It hung on a chain over the cabin table and was tied down to the table to keep it from swinging constantly with the boat's movement. Oh well! It wasn't the worst thing that could happen, just the loss of a bit of civilization. The day's run was 80 nautical miles.

Light air sails.

July 5. A day of squalls and little wind. We decided to motor for awhile. Gene managed to re-wind the starter and alternator and the engine started well enough but quit without a warning in the early afternoon. The small pre-filter was packed with fine particles of debris. Filter elements promised by Carl did not exist. I tried to start the engine again, but it fired on one cylinder briefly and then died. Several attempts resulted in same thing. Probably, the injectors were plugged up. I had been afraid of this. Later, when it was very calm, Gene and I would play with the injectors. There was a piece of small stainless steel wire in one of the tool boxes that I had used in the past to open the blocked hole of an injector. Meanwhile, we decided to heave to for the night since there was little or no wind. The day's run was 56 nautical miles.

July 6. Bill woke up at midnight last night and vainly tried to get Steve to help set sails. I think Steve was close to exhaustion from all that had happened recently. Actually, if you aren't used to being at sea just the constant motion can be very tiring. Steve was certainly willing to carry out his duties, but probably the hardest physical thing he did at home was to sit at his desk and answer the phone. He just wasn't ready for this level of physical stress. Bill waited impatiently until 8:35 am and then Steve rolled his tired body out of the bunk and helped to set sails. With the main up, we were off in a light, but steady new so'wester. I sewed sails all day except for taking the time to take a few sun sights. I had trouble getting a valid sight because of the cloud cover, but my line of position crossed my deduced reckoning line about 40 miles west of my deduced reckoning position. It seemed quite reasonable.

The next morning, **July 7**, ushered in a day of beautiful winds. We had a steady, moderate southwesterly until late afternoon when the wind picked up. We took in a reef as a matter of caution for the night to come, but it wasn't really needed. I sewed on the jib again. I had the big rip patched up and I was starting to rebuild the clew and leach. I thought it would be a light weather sail from then on to minimize the wear and tear. We would need it for getting into Papeete if we had to do it without an engine. The old sail we had been using was badly chafed and unreliable. The day's run was 121 nautical miles and we passed our first 1000 nautical miles total run.

July 8. Another day of good winds, but much as we appreciated making an easy passage, we were all tired of being wet and cold. We had been sailing mostly east rather than heading directly for Tahiti. This was to prevent us from being blown back too far when we got into the north-east trade winds and finding ourselves having to short tack our way to our destination. This was a regular routine in the days of the sailing ships. It was called making your easting. My noon sight put us further south than I thought we should be, about 120 nautical miles south of my deduced reckoning (DR). I decided to change our course more toward the north. Sailing at 30 degrees compass seemed about right. If this was maintained, it would take us straight to the Austral Islands, a group of islands that lay a little more than 300 nautical miles south of Tahiti. We would reach a milder climate soon where we could warm our spirits as well as our bodies. And the sight of land would reassure my crew.

Navigation was a great problem under the conditions we were in. It was too overcast most of the time to take sights. We could only get the Greenwich Time tick early in the morning and late in the afternoon. Taking accurate sights on a heavily rolling deck was next to impossible. We needed a place where the radio could be set up all the time for listening to the time tick. The sextant case needed to be altered so the telescope could be left in place instead of assembled each time it was used. It would have all helped!! These were silent complaints that kept rolling through my head, problems best kept to myself since there was nothing that could be done about them. I had to make do with what I had. The day's run was 123 nautical miles, almost the same as the day before.

July 9. I was tired and out of sorts. Any little thing that went wrong really irritated me, but I tried not to show it. I wondered why I was so edgy. I wasn't doing anything new that would require extra exertion. I hadn't stood a regular watch since the night of the big south wind. Gerard had taken my place so I could cook and navigate and, of course, sew sails as needed. I went to bed every night with the petrels—7 or 8 o'clock and didn't get up until 7 to start breakfast. I had the person coming off watch wake me up at the change of every watch and give me navigation details so I could make entries into the log, but I never had any trouble getting back to sleep, blessed sleep. Still, what tired me so? The constant motion? The physically unpleasant environment on the boat? Maybe it would be better when I could wash some things and get them dry. Maybe anxiety had something to do with it. I still hadn't fully recovered from the trauma of broaching. Then there were the leaking and the finicky pump and the engine problems. These things ate away at the time schedule I felt I needed to keep in order to have the boat in Hawaii in time for Max's schedule to work and also to keep my crew from thinking we were lost at sea. Now, at least the winds were with us. Except for the first few days, when we were blown almost all the way to Auckland and back, we had had fair winds. The last few days had been great — steady southwesterly winds. We were still headed straight for the Austral Islands. The day's run was 121 nautical miles.

July 10. I spent all morning taking and working out sun sights. I ran a series of morning sights and plotted them all out on the chart. I kept the ones that clustered well and threw out a couple that didn't. This was a technique I had read about in a navigation book that greatly improved the accuracy of my navigation. I then did a noon sight. This all brought us fairly close to our DR, although it indicated a rather large leeway to the south caused by wind or ocean currents. Probably this is what set us so far south on our previous course.

This afternoon was jib sewing time. I had been working on it for about four days, one stitch at a time with the big curved needle pushed through the cloth with the leather palm. I nearly had it finished. The mainsail had another small rip near the head from chafing. I'd sew some padding on it. I was really grateful that I brought my sail mending kit and extra sail cloth. We would have been in bad trouble without it. In the old days the sailing ships in-

Canvas bucket.

cluded a sailmaker in the crew. He spent his entire time making new sails, repairing old ones and making some practical items like canvas buckets. The canvas was usually made of linen and was much heavier than what I was working on. The sailmaker must have had strong hands and great patience.

Late in the day I was able to stow a nearly fully repaired sail in the sail bin that occupied part of the cabin in the bow and turned my attention to feeding four hungry sailors and my hungry self. We had Spanish rice for dinner. It was mushy, but had a good flavor. Anything to avoid the canned stew taste! Especially good things that I've managed to put together mostly from canned goods have been potato salad and canned franks, spaghetti, corned beef hash, curried shrimp and beans in spicy tomato sauce. The day's run was 130 nautical miles.

July 11. The grey days went on. I wondered where the tropics were. What was it like in Tahiti? Gene and I got into a conversation about Arizona. I was in the doghouse sewing stitch 300 or maybe 3000 on the jib and he was at the wheel with a cold spray belting him in the face. Arizona is dry and warm! A huge wave came over the bow and poured into every opening and into our bunks. How can so much water come through such small holes? A mystery! I dashed down below and shook my bedding desperately and mopped up with two half wet towels. Narhval is a leaker, top and bottom. Gene and I went back to talking and the conversation turned to restaurants. Marie Callender's for a piece of pecan pie. Some place like the Black Angus for a good steak or prime rib—6 nights straight. I realized suddenly that it was time to start dinner. "What would you like?" "Prime rib," he said. "Come on, Gene!" I smiled. "How about corned beef hash?"

Gene thinking of Arizona.

The day's run was 141 nautical miles. The total run from New Zealand was 1562 nautical miles.

The next day, **July 12**, was a repeat on the grey skies. None of us felt well. Even Bill has lost his good spirits. Gene had developed a painful sinus blockage and was put to bed with a dose of Dr. Steve's pills. I took his night watches and found them surprisingly enjoyable except for one incident. On the first watch I suddenly saw lights ahead. It was quite mysterious and rather frightening. Was it bioluminescence of some kind? Had I made some terrible navigational error and put us on a reef? I called Steve up and between us we determined that the lights were moving and that they belonged to a ship. It soon passed on toward the northwest, unknown forever.

Flying fish.

The first flying fish came aboard during Gerard's watch. He whooped and yelled with excitement and then mourned its escape. In the morning we found it in the bucket that had been left on deck filled with water. It was a small bony fish with big eyes and a lovely blue back. Flying fish don't really fly. They have a high dorsal fin that sets near the tail and a strong body. When chased by a predator they are able to leap powerfully from the surface of the water with the help of the large lower tail lobe and then use their long, wing-like pectoral fins to glide to safety. Some species have enlarged pelvic fins and are referred to as four-winged flying fish. In general, flying fish are capable of gliding to around 1000 feet by using the wave's updrafts, but typically their flights are much shorter. They are widely distributed in the world's oceans, but they are most commonly found in subtropical and tropical waters.

I wanted to throw the little fish back in the water and let it live its life of narrow escapes for awhile, but I was overruled by a crew hungry for fresh food and so it was served for dinner. It was only about 10 inches long so there were no more than a couple of bites for anyone, but it made for conversation and broke the monotony. These fish grow to about 12 inches so ours wasn't quite fully grown. Someone suggested that we might be coming into warmer waters since they are known for living in tropical and sub-tropical waters. We didn't have a thermometer, so it remained a likely guess. The day's run was 127 nautical miles.

July 13. The day had to be better and so it was! It was warmer, sunnier, calmer and happier. It was Bill's birthday and I was thinking about how we could celebrate it. We fished for mahi-mahi with some fishing gear that we found in one of the lockers where Karl had left some things and spent a lot of time on deck talking. Steve and Gerard got into some elaborate fantasies about food, especially pizza and chicken. I, too, yearned for some decent food, something fresh, some variety.

Just before dinner we celebrated Bill's birthday with a bag of goodies for him and a round of drinks for all hands. There was a good feeling of comradeship on the boat. The day's run was 115 nautical miles.

Pastel sunrise.

July 14. This was Narhval's second lovely calm day in a row, slipping along at 3-4 knots with genny and mule set. I suddenly remembered that it was Bastille Day, the French national holiday that commemorates an incident at the beginning of the French revolution. It happened in 1789 when a Paris mob stormed the Bastille, a prison, and released the prisoners, many of them political detainees. It was a strange thing to have entered my mind in the middle of the Pacific Ocean, but it gave me something to think about other than wind and water. The sunrise was brilliant and beautiful with clouds in delicate rainbow colors. The sunset was glorious, the sky filled with red and orange clouds as though on fire. I thought of the old rhyme.

> *Red sky at night,*
> *Sailor's delight.*
> *Red sky in the morning,*
> *Sailors take warning.*

We had all come to love ocean cruising in two good days, but I was certain it was a temporary sentiment. We all had baths, shampoos and general grooming. The men washed a few things and optimistically hung them on the line above the rail to dry. I baked several fragrant loaves of bread and made chili beans that were much too spicy. The crew was too nice to say much and even Bill, who came from a country with blandly seasoned food, managed to choke down a bowl. But, God they were hot!

I got a noon sight and a line of position (LOP), both snatched from between clouds. We hadn't had a single really clear day and I was impressed with the difficulty of celestial navigation, at least in these latitudes. Consequently, good deduced reckoning is very important. The taffrail log seemed pretty accurate so far in giving us distance through the water, but there was still that unaccountable directional error of about 15 degrees. I would see if it existed on the other tack when we got in the trade winds—in about 3-4 days, I hoped. The day's run was 100 nautical miles.

Small boat, big ocean.

July 15. We had the fortune to have a drying-out day that was warm, calm and welcome. The whole boat was draped with blankets, sleeping bags and clothing. We launched the dinghy and Bill rowed alongside and then ahead to take pictures. Even though we thought we were barely moving, it was difficult for Bill to keep up and quite a problem to get the dinghy back aboard.

I dried my blankets out and, although they became somewhat damp again when taken below, it was quite luxurious to have them over me for sleeping instead of the old mainsail which I had been sleeping under since the night we broached. It is very important to avoid getting seawater into clothing and bedding because it will remain soaking wet for weeks unless really warm sun is available for drying.

CABIN FEVER

I was becoming aware of what seemed to be some ill feeling brewing with the crew and wondered if it was directed toward me. I couldn't help wondering if it was because I was a woman, but maybe it was simply because I was the captain. It's hard to feel warmly toward someone who yells "All hands on deck!" in the middle of the cold night when you are getting some much needed sleep. And maybe doesn't show enough appreciation for your sacrifices. It was even more the case in the old days of the tall ships when the captains were usually much hated along with the mates. But, mutinies were a rare occurrence since, as a rule, the captain or the mariner, a ship's officer, were the only ones who knew how to navigate. Such was the case on our little ship with me as the only navigator. I was sorry about the problem, but there wasn't much I could do about it except to pretend I didn't notice. Maybe what I was sensing was people's reactions to the periodic rough seas, the wet boat, broken gear and general difficult conditions. You can't be expected to go around looking happy while sailing on a "hell ship" and my beloved Narhval was just that at times. The day's run was 93 nautical miles.

July 16. We passed two boats in the middle of the night last night. They were probably fishing boats. Tonight we passed buoys marking fishing lines. I thought they might be Japanese longlines. These lines have hundreds or even several thousand short lines with baited hooks attached along much of their length. Some are anchored at both ends so that they lie on the ocean floor where they catch bottom-dwelling fish like halibut and cod. Other types have floats that cause them to lie more on the surface of the sea and are used to catch tuna and swordfish. Unfortunately they may catch unintended prey like seabirds and dolphins and they are so efficient that they can deplete the fishing stocks.

The wind came up in the night and about 4 am we discovered that the mule halyard was loose aloft. We pulled it down and discovered that the head of the sail was pulled out. I had another sail mending job to do. By morning I was getting nervous over the genny. There is a motion that spells danger that I was becoming sensitive to. We took the genny down after breakfast and I was very happy with the easier motion. The speed diminished very little. I decided that a rule of thumb for the genny should be to take it down when whitecaps begin. It would save me a lot of sewing.

It was a typical day for me. I was up at 6 am to wash dishes from the night before and cook breakfast of potatoes, eggs, fruit, bread and butter. The bread had been baked the day before. Then I helped to change sails, took a morning sun sight, brought the DR up to date, worked out the sun sight and did the dishes from breakfast. The men were bravely willing to stand a watch in the middle of a stormy night and would even crawl out on the bowsprit to free a sail, but I couldn't get them to do the dishes. So, after the dishes were stacked to dry in a secure rack on the galley sink, I worked out a prediction for a noon sight from our DR, took the sight and worked it out. Then I made lunch, cleaned up again and made four loaves of bread, a tedious process with the little portable oven that I set on top of the kerosene stove. It was kept from flying off the stove by securing it with some wire that was kept handy. I set one loaf out on deck with some butter as soon as it had cooled and the crew happily demolished it. The others were saved for regular meals. Then, it was time to cook dinner and clean up. All of this while struggling constantly to keep from falling over or dropping things with the rolling and pitching of the boat. I managed to read *Sand Pebbles* for awhile before going to sleep. It's an interesting novel about a real American gun boat named the San Pablo patrolling on the Yangtze River before World War II. We had several of these boats in China to protect American interests. I once knew a man who had served aboard one of these vessels, which added a personal meaning to the book. The day's run was 74 nautical miles. The total run from New Zealand was 2053 nautical miles (2361 statute miles).

July 17. Bill says that strange or dangerous things always happen in the middle of the night and so they have. Last night was the strangest night happening of the trip. About 2 o'clock Bill was on watch and Steve was visiting with him although Steve's watch had ended at midnight. They had got into a conversation so stimulating that Steve just stayed on. They were steering due north with the wind slightly heading us on the port beam. The stars were out, but the moon was dark. They were so intently concentrating on their verbal exchange that they were unaware of a huge black cloud bearing down on them until it was right before them. It had a wide expanse and reached vertically from the high in the sky to the surface of the water except for a tunnel placed directly before them through which they could see the starlit water beyond. They sailed through the tunnel, their skins crawling and the hair of their necks rising. At the end of the tunnel the wind suddenly switched and the boat jibed over. What caused this change? Were we suddenly in the trade winds? Bill was especially affected by this eerie happening and talked excitedly about it for some time before he could quiet down enough to go to sleep. He described it as being like a passage into another life. He suggested that whenever anything unusual like this happens we should wake everyone so they could share in the experience. I deeply regretted not seeing it and thought about it all the next day trying to imagine what it was like. Later, I found a photograph in my collection from another place and time that

Mysterious cloud.

seemed to match Bill's description. The day's run was 127 nautical miles.

July 18. Yesterday the wind fell steadily all day until the sails were slatting and the blocks and boom were banging with each roll of the boat. I don't know of a more irritating sound or motion. Being becalmed, as we were, really added to the frustration. Gene and Steve took it good naturedly with Gerard falling in with them. Bill and I became quite irritable and came close to our first conflict of authority. So far, we had a pretty good arrangement considering his superior sail-handling ability and my role as skipper. We both had alpha personalities and there was also the matter of gender roles which I refused to follow. Bill always brought his ideas about sail changes to me in a seemingly offhanded way, not like he was asking for authorization. If I agreed, he ordered the sail change and directed the operation. I might have taken the wheel if needed, but I didn't interfere. He really knew what he was doing and had great leadership ability. He had always been a good sport when I disagreed with him. I tried to keep it as a suggestion or a request rather than an order. Several times I showed some really bad judgment on things I asked him to do and he never criticized me openly.

Yesterday afternoon he completely ignored me and discussed his plans with the others. They tried one thing after another—booming the sails out, taking them in, and even setting the genny to fly like a spinnaker. Nothing helped. We were down to one knot. Sails flailed wildly with the swells. I asked him to take down everything and forget it. "What do you blokes think about trying the other tack?" he said to Gene and Steve without looking at me. Confronting him would do no good and would probably make matters even worse. I gritted my teeth and kept my mouth shut until about 5:30. I was baking cinnamon rolls and Bill came below and went into raptures about the good smells from the galley. I showed him a potato salad I had just made. "I'm working hard to fix you all a good dinner, but I'm really in a bad mood from being becalmed." "So am I!" he said. "I can't stand not moving!" I turned to him with the pan of cinnamon rolls in my hand and said quietly, "If you wouldn't mind too much I'd like to have the sails taken down before dark so we can all have dinner together." Food won out! "Righty Oh" he sang out in his wonderful kiwi style and went on deck to douse the sails.

Close to morning, I was awakened from a sound sleep. It was Bill calling my name softly, "There's a lovely breeze come up. I've got coffee perking. Will ya have a cuppie?" Sleepiness dragged at my judgment, but I realized that we were back to our amenable arrangement and I had better not disregard it. We shared a pleasant short interval over coffee and then I thought of the good wind that was going to waste. "Let's get the main and jib up," I suggested. "Righty Oh! Get up mates! We're setting sail for Tahiti!" When we woke up enough we all caught some of Bill's spirit and the night took on an element of excitement. The sails came up against a star-studded sky and we headed for the magic tropical islands.

LAND AHEAD

At about 10 am we saw several white, very long-tailed birds flying overhead. I thought they were tropicbirds, a sign we were getting into tropical waters. Tropicbirds are pelagic birds that spend their entire lives on tropical and subtropical seas except for times of mating and raising chicks on isolated islands. They look a little like gulls with white feathers and a few black markings. They are about the same size as gulls, but what distinguishes them is the extremely long, narrow tail extension that is formed from the central feathers of the tail. They are unable to walk on land because their webbed feet are placed almost at the end of their bodies to facilitate swimming. So, they move on land by pushing with their feet and gliding along on their bellies. They are said to make rare appearances around the Channel Islands off the coast of Southern California, but I have never seen them there. Frigate birds also have very long tails and may occur in tropical waters, but the males are all black except for an inflatable red neck pouch that makes them irresistible to females during breeding season. The females are mostly black with some white patches. Those would be the wrong colors for the white bird we sighted. I would have loved to have seen a frigate bird since they are unusual in many ways. They are seemingly made for flight with the largest wing area compared to their body weight of any bird. Their bones are mostly filled with air, which makes them unusually light, and their pectoral muscles are highly developed. This allows them to stay in the air for several weeks at a time although they may also land on islands for the night. They fly over the water to look for food rather than landing or swimming in the water. The reason for this is that their feathers are not water repellant and they are unable to take off from the water as most pelagic birds do. Their prey is mostly small fish or squid. These may be taken from just below the surface of the water or snatched from the air in the case of flying fish leaping from the water to escape larger prey. They also snatch food away from other birds or steal chicks from other bird's nests. In Hawaii they are known as the iwa (thief) bird. I tend to think of them as bad birds, but I guess it isn't rational to place human values on the behavior of birds.

The day's run was 46 nautical miles. I was surprised we made that much distance with such light winds most of the time. It really paid to keep as much sail up as possible in light air.

July 19. I went to bed last night with much anxiety because I had predicted that we would soon sight Ra'ivavae, one of the Austral Islands that lie south of Tahiti. The Australs are the southernmost part of the French collectivity (territory) of Polynesia. They consist of five habitable islands, including Ra'ivavae and also several uninhabited ones. They are grouped into two archipelagos. The northern archipelago, which included Ra'ivavae, is the largest. It would be our first landfall in over 2000 nautical miles on the first trip I had ever navigated at sea out of sight of land. I worked on navigation most of the day yesterday taking morning, noon and afternoon sights. I averaged the last of the five shots. I played with the DR trying to pin down what seemed like an easterly error. Then I made some bold and confident-sounding statements after Bill said in a put-up-or-shut-up tone of voice "When do you expect to sight the island, Anne?" Dividers in hand, the chart laid out, I did a 5-knot estimate. "We should be abeam of the island sometime between 7 and 8 tomorrow morning if we maintain our speed. Let's be sure to keep a good look out all night just to be on the safe side." "7:30, then?" he said, pinning me down further. "Yes!"

Most of the Austral Islands are high islands with outlying coral reefs rather than atolls, which consist only of a reef bordering a lagoon. High islands are actually mountains rising from the sea floor and are the remains of volcanic activity from long ago. If the waters surrounding the island are warm enough coral will grow and form a reef around the island. Corals are small invertebrate animals in the form of polyps that live in colonies. They secrete calcium carbonate that forms a hard protective shell around the colony that we call coral. Many of these shells fused together form coral reefs. An atoll is formed when, over long periods of time, the island erodes away or subsides and disappears completely, leaving the coral reef surrounding a lagoon. Coral reefs are only found in the warm waters of tropical and sub-tropical sea. Generally speaking they lie between 30 degrees N and 30 degrees S latitudes. The optimum temperature for most corals is 26 to 16 degrees Celsius. Most corals depend on getting up to 90 percent of their energy from a symbiotic relationship with single-celled plant-like organisms called dinoflagellates that are photosynthetic and can produce energy from sunlight. These organisms live within the tissues of the coral polyps and furnish the various colors found in healthy corals. They and their coral hosts can only live at water depths that allow sufficient sunlight to penetrate for photosynthesis. In clear water this is about 200 feet (60 m). If certain stressful conditions occur the coral will expel the dinoflagellates as a short-term way of survival. The coral loses its color and is said to have become bleached. It will starve if the situation is not reversed soon and eventually the reef will erode and collapse. Rising ocean temperature caused by global climate change with resulting lower ocean oxygen content

A coral skeleton.

is thought to be the present major cause of this destruction. It is now becoming widespread in tropical and subtropical areas.

In 1789, Tubuai, one of the Austral Islands, was the location for the first refuge of the Bounty mutineers. Fletcher Christian, the leader of the mutiny, knew they couldn't go back to Tahiti because the British authorities would be looking for them so they sailed south to these little-known islands. The native islanders were very hostile and there were serious conflicts. The mutineers wanted to establish a permanent settlement on Tubuai, but lacked enough people and there were no women with them. They sailed back to Tahiti and with a certain amount of trickery they got almost 30 Tahitian men and women to return to Tubuai. They worked on constructing a fort, but there were constant conflicts with the natives and discontentment among the mutineers. Most of them wanted to go back to Tahiti and take their chances there. Christian agreed, the Bounty sailed back to Tahiti once more, deposited all but eight of the mutineers, tricked more Tahitians aboard, especially women, and sailed away to the remote island of Pitcairn where some of their descendants still live.

In spite of interesting thoughts about mutineers of long ago the evening was tedious. In a desperate move to have something fresh tasting I had put raw onions in the four-bean salad that I had made for dinner and my stomach was beginning to rumble. I know that I can't eat raw onions without getting indigestion, but I went ahead and did it anyway. I was very late with my bread making because I had played navigator for too long so there was still the little baker's task to be done. The trade winds were really with us now and the motion was such that I had to stand in the galley with potholders in hand almost the entire two hours that it took to bake four loaves of bread to be ready to catch the oven if it threatened to fly off the stove top. I had a wire preventer around the bottom of the damn thing, but it wasn't foolproof. Just before the first pan of bread was due to come out the wind swung to the east and the crew decided to jibe over. I ran out and took the wheel for the operation which always seemed like a minor emergency with the main boom whipping with sudden force to the other side of the boat and the other sails following with a bit less violence. Soon done, I dashed below, snatched the pan out of the oven with a slight finger scorching and tossed the next pan into the oven. Gerard, who had been waiting all day for the bread, was at my elbow and Gene was at Gerard's elbow. We sliced up a loaf, fragrant with the smell of raisins and of the bread itself. Accompanied with good New Zealand butter, strawberry jam and hot coffee it was just in time for the change of the watch. The open signs of satisfaction and gratitude were a great reward for my efforts. This pleased me, but I still went to bed nervous about the sighting of the islands.

As I lay in my bunk, a swarm of anxieties raced through my head. What if we were closer than I thought and we hit the island? Although there was no moon the stars were out and gave some light. Most of the habitable islands in the archipelago are high islands and the tallest is over 1500 feet. Everyone swore they would be able to see it. No problem. Well, what if we missed it entirely? The crew would lose confidence in me as a navigator and my authority would slip. I slept fitfully, but each time I dozed off I dreamed in brilliant images of small high islands surrounded by motus, coral reefs covered with waving palms. In between dreams I listened for what is sometimes described in books as "the sound of surf booming on the reefs". Or I heard bits of conversation from people on watch. "No, I can't see a thing. The horizon is absolutely clear."

Steve woke me at 6 am as always, so I could start breakfast. I went on deck with Steve and Gene and we all took a long look at the horizon and the rising sun. About 7 am Steve sang out "There it is!" And there was Ra'ivavae right on schedule—ragged peaks coming up out of the sea about 10 miles away slightly off the starboard quarter. We called for Bill and Gerard to come and share the moment. I asked the crew if they would like to pay the island a short visit. If we got closer maybe someone would come out in a fishing boat and show us the way through the main pass in the reef. They looked at me in astonishment, like I was trying to lead them into further danger and all agreed to go on by and get to Tahiti as quickly as possible. I was disappointed, but said nothing. Bill and I both broke out secret supplies of liquor and all hands were given a glass. Steve even had a cigar from his secret supply with his rum. We all looked at the chart. I was formally

There are the Australs. The island of Ra'ivavae barely shows up as a streak of land on the horizon.

congratulated and we all rejoiced. Gene said that it should be called happy day instead of Friday. These were people who had gone on a trip across the ocean with a woman who said she could navigate, but had not demonstrated it until now after we had sailed almost 2500 nautical miles without sighting land. They must have begun to wonder if they had signed on with the devil. But, today I had proven my worth and it was official. I was now Navigator Belovich and I happily set a course for Tahiti. The day's run was 109 nautical miles. Total distance run = 2333 nautical miles.

July 20. The wind came around more to the east late yesterday and made for a very uncomfortable ride last night. Crash, bang, sloppp! The waves were hitting almost on the beam. I had unkind words for whoever it was who cut my nice, high bunk board down in the middle so that my rear end sagged out on a starboard tack. I wasn't in danger of falling out of my bunk, but it was pretty uncomfortable. The wind settled down somewhat after daybreak and the morning was overcast with a layer of clouds that looked dark and squally in some directions. The air and water were much warmer now. We were still wearing oilskins on watch to keep from getting wet, but finding them a little too warm, even with the wind blowing. No one was complaining. It was wonderful to be warm after having been cold for so long.

I saw a whale leap partly out of the water, turn and hit the water on its back. It was almost black and had some flashes of white on the tail. I was astonished that it could leap like that because it appeared to be about 40 or 50 feet long. It happened so quickly that I couldn't alert anyone else to look in time. I thought it must be a humpback whale because they were known to be in those waters at this time of year. Humpbacks are baleen whales that feed on small fish and on krill, small crustaceans that swim in the open sea. They are called humpbacks because they curve their backs more than other whales when they dive. The males are noted for their long and interesting songs that seem to be a way of interacting with other whales. The whales in any particular area all sing the same song, but the song is different in each major area. The hunting of these whales is closely restricted by the International Whaling Commission and some countries have given them additional protection. There are large areas of humpback-protected waters around the Hawaiian Islands.

I set a course of 340 degrees yesterday after passing the island and finding that we were creeping too far over to the west. This morning I began wondering if the navigational error was caused by making leeway with the wind coming around to the east. Bill confessed that he had been steering 340 degrees all night before I ordered the change. I was really annoyed. It sure made deduced-reckoning a problem when the crew changed the course to please themselves, but since Bill was probably right, I couldn't say much. 340 degrees it was.

I was beginning to have some concern about getting into Papeete without engine power. I studied the charts and sailing directions. It didn't look easy, but if Captain Cook could get Endeavor in there on his way to Matavai Bay where he observed the transit of Venus across the sun in 1769, I guess we could manage Narhval. Endeavor was a full-rigged ship that was nearly 100 feet long and didn't have an engine. Of course the native people had been sailing in and out of the harbor for centuries. Their voyaging vessels were large, even by today's standards. Some were over 100 feet long, but most were somewhat smaller. They were usually multihulled, fitted as outriggers or catamarans and were held together by platform-like decks that were equipped with roofed shelters for the crew and passengers and places for food storage. The masts carried distinctive claw-shaped sails and many were capable of tacking into the wind. Most of them were built by lashing planking together with locally made small cordage and caulking the seams with native materials rather than hollowing out single logs like the natives of the American Pacific Northwest did in building their sea-going canoes.

Europeans sailing through the South Pacific have reported sighting various islands that are now part of French Polynesia since the 16th Century, but it wasn't until the 18th Century that any of them actually visited one. Cook was an early visitor along with some French, Spanish and Dutch explorers. Cook was especially fortunate in meeting a native navigator named Tupaia who drew a sort of primitive chart of the islands that aided him greatly in exploring that part of the Pacific. The early European explorers of the South Pacific islands were amazed at the natives' ability to find their way from one island to another without charts or navigation instruments, even though they were many miles apart. Most of the courses steered took the crew out of the sight of land with only a view of the sky and open sea to guide them. Part of the secret to this remarkable skill was an intimate relationship with the natural elements from early childhood on. They lived much of their lives out-of-doors and a good share of their livelihood came from the sea. They knew which way the winds blew, the clouds moved and the ocean swells traveled. They knew how far out to sea certain birds

French flag.

could be seen. There was also a formal, long-held tradition of passing the skills of navigation down orally from one generation to the next. Becoming a navigator was based on acquiring extensive knowledge of patterns of movement and positions of the sun, stars, winds, ocean swells, ocean phosphorescence and behavior of sea native birds. Instruction began in childhood and continued into adulthood with more and more challenging lessons including actual voyages to distant islands.

The primary method of navigating involved steering by the stars. It came as a surprise to me to learn that, although stars rise at different times throughout the year, they always rise and set at the same place with slight differences depending on the latitude of the voyager. The islanders knew where to look along the horizon for the right star to mark the heading for their destination. Some stars guided them directly toward their goal while others were to be lined up by the helmsman with certain parts of the rigging or other parts of the boat. Since most stars move as an arc in the sky rather than passing directly overhead, each guiding star was useful only when it was low in the horizon, either as it was rising or setting. When it rose

Tahiti ahead.

too high to be useful the navigator would select another lower guiding star to follow. This would be repeated with as many new stars as were needed.

As the destination island drew closer there would be other signs to look for. I remember seeing tropic birds as we approached the Austral Islands south of Tahiti and wondering how far out from land they might be seen. The islanders knew the habits of each species and just how far from land they would fly and would note the direction they flew to reach land late in the day. They also watched the ocean swells to see if there were any counter swells crossing the main pattern. This would indicate swells hitting the island destination and bouncing back. It took a much-practiced eye to detect them. Observing clouds could be helpful, too. They tended to move differently and have different colors and shapes when they were over land rather than over the sea.

Tahiti closer.

The London Missionary Society, a Protestant organization, set up the first permanent settlement in Tahiti in 1797. French Catholic missionaries arrived in 1834. There were conflicts between the Catholic missionaries and the Polynesians who had converted to Protestantism and France sent a ship to protect the missionaries. In 1842 Tahiti and another island were claimed as a French Protectorate. In 1880 France declared Tahiti a colony with Papeete as the capital. Other islands were taken in by France and are known collectively as French Polynesia. After World War II the Polynesians were given French citizenship with the right to vote and the Protectorate was changed to a French Territory. In 2003, the status of territory was changed to a collectivity with much more autonomy. French Polynesia is made up of the Society Islands, which include Tahiti and Moorea, the Austral Islands, the Tuamotus, the Marquesas and the Gambiers. We could expect to find the French in charge when we reached Papeete. The day's run was 138 nautical miles.

July 21. We sighted The Society Islands many hours earlier than I had predicted. There seemed to be an error of between 40 and 50 miles. I thought it might have been a taffrail log error, but since the log behaved perfectly from Tahiti to Tetiaroa, maybe it was a current pushing us along. Another possibility, which I later decided was the most likely, was that because the spinner of the taffrail log kept jumping out of the water frequently in the heavy chop we had sailed through since leaving the Australs, it would not have measured an accurate distance through the water.

End of Bill's voyage.

Bill and I had a series of minor arguments the rest of the way. I wanted to keep somewhat to the east of the island to be sure we didn't get set over by the strong trade winds and miss it. He wanted to close in. We compromised. What he thought was the island of Moorea I thought was the island of Tahiti. It turned out that I was right and it must have irritated him. He thought I was sailing too close to the reef. We were a good 3 to 4 miles from the island and the chart showed the reef only a mile out. He wouldn't look at the chart. His man-first personality said loudly that he needed to be in charge, not this "know-it-all" woman. It was lucky that his part of the trip was coming to an end before we got into a major conflict of some kind. Of course, I would miss the cheerfulness and willingness that he showed during most of the voyage and would seriously miss his sailing skills. Furthermore, I really liked him and wanted to maintain a friendship. The stresses of the trip made it very difficult at times.

Steve was writing in his journal while I was doing the dishes in the galley next to his bunk. The galley floor was a step higher than the main cabin. This put the journal right in front of my eyes. I couldn't help reading his plans to jump ship in Tahiti. My God, what a shock! I almost blurted out my concern, but I needed his help to get the boat to Hawaii and didn't want to alienate him, so I said nothing. I hoped he would dry out, warm up, change his mind and continue on.

ISLANDS OF PARADISE AND A NEW CREW

Approaching the lush, verdant, ethereal island of Tahiti in a small boat after sailing thousands of miles across a cold and wave-lashed sea is an experience that is hard to adequately describe. It is a high island with sharply rising, pyramid-shaped volcanic peaks. Mount Orohena is over 7,000 feet. The scalloped feet of the mountains sink directly into the sea with coastal plains to be seen only in a few places. The land is surrounded by a narrow fringing reef and a small lagoon. This indicates that the island is relatively new in geological time compared to Society Islands like Bora Bora, which has a much larger reef and lagoon and a smaller land mass that has been worn away or subsided over a long period of time. I was so excited about reaching land after such a long time at sea and enthralled with the view that I insisted on steering most of the night and all of the next morning. We were maddeningly slow getting to Papeete because first the wind dropped and then, after daybreak, it came around Venus Point with a vengeance and headed us. We tacked way out to the north of Moorea on a course calculated to make it into the harbor entrance on the next tack. After that, it was really easy except for Bill wanting to have his way about everything, his last chance for rebelling against my authority and showing everyone who was boss. We short tacked up the harbor past the yachts that were tied to the quay, and then came back so we were directly out from an empty slot where we dropped the anchor, dropped the sails and backed in with the help of the dinghy and some long lines. Narhval was tied up to the quay stern first along with many other boats large and small, mostly sailing yachts from foreign ports.

A gendarme came aboard almost immediately and asked some official questions. How long did I plan to stay? Who were the crew members and where were they from? Did I have any weapons aboard? He told me that I would have to take

Coming in to Papeete.

Anne with the Sailing Illustrated people.

the shotgun that Carl Putz had left on the boat to the police station right away. I would be able to retrieve it when I was ready to leave. I walked to the station, not too far away, as directed, while carrying the shotgun. It was in a case, but still obviously a gun and it made me feel very conspicuous and self-conscious. What if someone was puzzled and alarmed to see a sunburned, tousle-haired woman in sailing clothes walking through the streets of Papeete carrying a shotgun and decided to take action. I tried to rehearse what I might say if someone thought I looked dangerous and confronted me. The Polynesians had never completely accepted the rule of the French and there were always whispers of rebellion. Possession of firearms by citizens was illegal. Maybe I would be seen as a conspirator. I was greatly relieved that I made it the whole way and no one seemed to notice anything unusual.

Not long after docking, Bill's wife, Esme arrived to join him for a vacation. I was pleased to see her and greeted her warmly. She backed away with such coldness that I was shocked. Was she imagining something? Was it something Bill had told her? Perhaps he had complained to her about my being too authoritarian. Did she simply resent his sailing with another woman? I was never to know, but always regretted it because she had been so nice to us in New Zealand and I really liked her.

I got a much better reception from some people who worked for the yachting magazine, *Sailing Illustrated*. They were interested in the boat and our trip and wanted to do an article. I forgot about it for awhile and never made any further inquiries so I don't know if it was ever published.

Then, I learned that Gene and Gerard wanted to leave the boat as well as Steve. Since Bill had come aboard with the agreement that he would go only as far as Tahiti, this would leave me without any crew whatsoever. I spent the night mostly lying awake with a lot of desperate thoughts running through my head about possibly single-handing the boat to Hawaii. By morning, not only had I come to my senses and acknowledged that it would be impossible to single-hand with a boat like Narhval, but I was somewhat relieved to learn that Bill had talked Gerard into going on. Gene and Steve asked me what I was

Gerard, loyal sailor.

going to do about a crew. I told them that the gendarme who had visited the boat right after we docked had told me that I would have to go to the police station and sign for any crew members who wanted to permanently leave the boat. I decided to drive a hard bargain and agreed to sign for them only if they found replacements for the three of them who were leaving. This didn't go over very well, and somehow, I seemed to be blamed, but they went into immediate action, finding materials to make a large sign saying "Crew Needed" and fastening it to the stern of the boat where it was clearly visible from the path along the quay.

In the days of the old sailing ships the missing crew would have been replaced by paying a boarding master (crimp) "blood money" to trick some sailors in to signing on to serve on the ship. This was known as crimping or shanghaiing. A common method was to feed a man enough rum to incapacitate him, sometimes to make him unconscious. Then he would be taken aboard the ship and his name

Narhval docked at Papeete.

would be forged on the ship's articles. Once he was signed aboard it was illegal for him to leave before the end of the voyage. It was actually a form of temporary slavery by which a crimp could earn the equivalent of several hundred thousand dollars per year. Here are several verses of the old sea chanty that tells it well.

What shall we do with a drunken sailor?
What shall we do with a drunken sailor?
What shall we do with a drunken sailor?
Early in the morning?
Way-hay, up she rises
Way-hay, up she rises
Way-hay, up she rises
Early in the morning
Put him in the long boat 'til he's sober
Put him in the long boat 'til he's sober
Put him in the long boat 'til he's sober
Way-hay, up she rises
Way-hay, up she rises
Way-hay, up she rises
Early in the morning

Yachts along the quay.

I preferred a gentler method and in a short time I had three new voluntary crew members. I wrote the departing crew letters of release for the immigration authorities. We went to the police station together with the letters where, unfortunately, our final parting was not as cordial as I would have wished, but was as I should have expected.

The new soon-to-be sailors were David Bryant, British subject, athlete, bit-part movie actor and stunt man from Hollywood; Harry Morton, high school math teacher from Glendale, California on sabbatical leave; and his very bright teen-age son, Russ Morton. They all seemed like very good people and I was deeply grateful to have their volunteer service. I owed David's presence to the fact that he had stayed in Tahiti until he ran out of money. There may have been a romantic reason behind this somewhat irrational action. Before we sailed away he took a

Tahiti scene.

short afternoon leave to go and tell someone goodbye. I imagined it was a beautiful Tahitian girl. I thought that Harry Morton wanted the sailing experience and the adventure that came with it, a surprising thing for the ordinary sort of person he seemed to be. If you bought a tract house in the suburbs he would be the very nice next-door neighbor who always kept his lawn mowed and his Ford sedan clean. As it turned out there was actually a lot more strength to his character than that.

My longtime friends Jerry Taylor and Evie Frisel arrived in their little boat, Puffin, in the middle of the week and did everything possible to help me. Most of the first part of the week had been spent in a nightmare of searching for a marine diesel mechanic. With the help of Jean Pierre, Jerry and Eve's Chinese friend, I finally found a good one who quickly put the engine back in running condition. Jean Pierre also loaned me enough money to pay for the repair. What an amazing act of kindness! I had worried a great deal about the engine, about getting the boat ready in other ways and about money. It was a blessed rescue that allowed me to relax once more and regain my confidence. To add to this happy situation Evie drove me around to see some of the island in a car they rented. It was a time when I really needed friends and they were among the best.

Gene and Steve made a quick visit back to the boat. They were still waiting to get seats on a plane to take them home. I didn't ask them where they were staying, but it was evidently not in a hotel because they really needed to use the head (marine toilet). They managed to plug it up and I spent the afternoon taking it apart and cleaning it on the deck. It was lucky I knew how to do it.

After the engine was fixed I took the new, inexperienced crew out and gave them their first sailing lesson and showed them how to read the compass. We practiced reefing sails and I made sure that everyone understood the importance

Tahiti, inland.

Le truck.

of tying a square knot that could be untied easily instead of a granny knot that might stubbornly refuse to open, especially when it was wet. Together we chanted "right over left and left over right" to remind them of how the knot was properly tied. I thought they did very well considering that none of them had ever sailed before. We made plans for where each person would sleep and when they would stand their watches. Sailing harnesses were passed out with strict instructions about keeping a safety line secured while under way. My greatest nightmare was having someone fall overboard. It is slow and difficult to turn a big sailboat completely around and sail back on a reverse course and almost impossible to see someone floating in a sea filled with big waves.

David and I walked to the big outdoor market for supplies. People zoomed by on motorbikes and now and then one of the open-air buses locally referred to as les trucks would lumber past. I thought the supplies were somewhat expensive, but we couldn't go without them. Besides, it was wonderful to be able to get some fresh food, especially the tropical fruit. David had a romantic idea that we should sail off with a bunch of bananas in the rigging and I went along with it to keep him happy. I picked up the shotgun on the way back to the boat and carried it the rest of the way with the same trepidation as before. Harry had located some kerosene, the fuel required for the stove and some straight grain alcohol to prime it for starting. The alcohol was in a bottle that looked like it was for human consumption and made me wonder about the drinking habits of the natives. We put our supplies away and were ready for the new voyage the next day. I tried to imagine what my new crew members were thinking that night. Did they have any idea of what it meant to sail across the ocean for over 2500 nautical miles? They would keep going day and night through wind and calm, steering the boat and tending the sails in a rhythmic pattern. At least, it wouldn't be cold like it was on the first part of the trip from New Zealand.

THE ANCHOR IS WEIGHED

July 30. I woke up humming the old sea chanty "Away Rio" to myself.

> *O, the anchor is weighed, and the sails they are set,*
> *Away, Rio!*
> *The maids that we're leaving we'll never forget,*
> *For we're bound for the Rio Grande,*
> *And away, Rio! aye, Rio!*
> *Sing fare-ye-well, my bonny young gel,*
> *For we're bound for the Rio Grande!*
>
> *We've a jolly good ship, and a jolly good crew,*
> *Away, Rio!*
> *A jolly good mate, and a good skipper, too,*
> *For we're bound for the Rio Grande,*
> *And away, Rio! aye, Rio!*
> *Sing fare-ye-well, my bonny young gel,*
> *For we're bound for the Rio Grande!*

Getting under way to leave paradise was totally uneventful and almost dreamlike. Jerry and Evie waved goodbye from the shore as we motored out. The weather was calm and the scenery was spectacular. The green vegetation that covered the island seemed especially brilliantly colored against the blue of the sky. I hoped to be able to return to the charming little city of Papeete with my husband, Max, someday under better circumstances. We powered all the way to Tetiaroa to get away from the irregular winds around the island and to give us a good start in

Evie waving goodbye.

the light airs. The new crew had no trouble steering and immediately took over the night watches. There was a wonderful feeling of congeniality on the boat. The wind went around slightly to the south and I thought we would be able to make our necessary easting to 145 W longitude while we were sailing in the southeast trade winds. This was necessary in order to avoid beating into the wind with frequent tacking to get to Hawaii when we crossed the doldrums and reached the northeast trade winds. I expected a good trip.

12:45 pm we started the McCulloch, our small gas engine, and hooked it up to the battery charger. It seemed to be charging well. Off at 1:55. It was up to about a three-quarter charge.

July 31. All morning the weather was just like the movies of the South Seas with big, lovely, fluffy clouds. We were gliding over blue water with 10 knots of wind in the sails. David's bunch of bananas in the rigging was just beginning to ripen. Around noon we took the jib down and raised the genny. There isn't anything quite like a little speed to raise everyone's spirits. It seemed like a different boat—dry, warm, stable and light.

August 1. Good weather continued. The crew learned the new routines very quickly. There was some minor seasickness and fatigue. Russ was very bright and responsible. He started the generator every day and checked the batteries. Before we left Papeete he disconnected the terrible cobweb of wiring that existed in the boat and left only the center compass and the navigation lights. We ran only the compass light routinely. The bulb was much too bright. We had to tape over it to keep from being blinded and it drew too much electricity. We thought we would have to run the generator ½ hour per day to keep up with it. That used ¼ gallon of gas. We started out with 5 gallons of gas, just barely enough. We could run short. I decided to recommend that Max take 10 gallons for the trip from Hawaii.

Maybe the alternator hookup to the diesel engine, which had never worked, could be repaired in Hawaii.

I fooled around with navigation a lot. It entertained me and helped the time pass. We were making fair progress and sufficient easting, although none to spare. Everything was going so well that I was able to completely relax for the first time on the trip and really enjoy the sailing.

Leaving Tahiti.

The wind was light to moderate all day and the sky was filled with scattered good weather clouds. The crew put the genny up this afternoon and it was a sort of a snafu. Gerard tried to direct the operation, but although he is an excellent sailor he is too nonverbal by nature to clearly pass directions on to the rest of the crew. The sail wasn't laid out properly, got caught on the anchor winch and was damaged. I spent half an hour patching it. I tried to be good natured, but made it clear that Gerard should take the wheel if I was on watch. He would do an excellent job of keeping the boat heading the right way and I would direct the foredeck operations. The day's run was 96 nautical miles.

August 2. We made good progress during the night, but woke to a day with a completely different look about it. It was overcast with a rising wind. About 7:00 this morning the genny came loose at the foot and I yelled for all hands on deck to get it down before it was torn to pieces. The routine was smartly handled and it turned out that the shackle had broken rather than the tack splice being torn out as I had feared. The sail was soon back, but had to be replaced by the jib within an hour because of rising wind. Just before noon, Gerard shouted down the hatch that we should reef the main. I agreed and we had another "All hands on deck". This was the new crew's first reefing at sea and I thought it went fairly well. I was glad we had practiced before starting the voyage because otherwise it could have turned into a Marx Brothers routine with Groucho at the helm. Briefly it went like this: 1. Take up on the topping lift to relieve the pressure on the sail. 2. Come

Sailing wing and wing.

into the wind briefly, raise the boom with a shoulder and secure the boom with the boom lift. 3. Lower the sail while taking in on the luff line. 4. Simultaneously or immediately take in on the leach line (block and tackle on the boom). 5. Tie the reef pennants with square knots. The strain on the lines should be equal, but the knots don't need to be really tight. As the wind continued to rise we also lowered the mizzen. I thought that the crew deserved a special recognition for the day's outstanding performance. I praised them with enthusiasm and, even better, I made a batch of chocolate chip cookies and presented it to be devoured on the spot. The day's run was 103 nautical miles.

August 3. We sailed all night with jibs and reefed main, making a good 5 knots average. The motion was uncomfortable and the boat took on a lot of water. It had to be pumped for about 20 minutes every two hours. We now had a rule that each person coming off watch must pump the bilge dry. Otherwise, some people never pump much and resentment builds.

David was nervous about the squalls at night, understandably since it was a new experience and they seemed pretty threatening. We doused the main for the first one partly to relieve David's anxiety and partly for prudence. After a while we decided that there wasn't really that much meanness in it so we upped the main again for the rest of the night. I have been told that squalls are the strongest when they come out of a black cloud in the middle of a clear sky. The doldrums are much squallier than this area and we'll need to be ready for them. The day's run was 134 nautical miles.

August 4. I baked bread for my new crew for the first time today and they were duly impressed. The routine was to put the dough together, knead it and then let it rise while taking the noon sight and getting lunch. Then, I baked it in the afternoon before taking the afternoon sight and getting dinner ready. I always made enough dough for 4 loaves and baked two at a time in the little portable oven that I put on top of the kerosene stove. When the first two loaves had risen in the pan I would light both of the burners on the stove, wire the oven to the top and heat it to 375 degrees by the built-in thermometer. While the loaves were baking I would shape the other two and let them rise in the pan ready to be baked in turn. Having fresh bread and butter at sea always seemed almost like a miracle. At about 6 am the wind had dropped sufficiently and we shook the reef out of the main. At 2 pm we raised the genny.

The day's run was 115 nautical miles. Total run from New Zealand was 3208 nautical miles. This was equal to about 3680 regular statute miles.

August 5. The wind blew steadily all day and small clouds passed overhead with absolute regularity. We were making good progress, chewing up about 2 degrees of latitude each day and making fair easting, somewhat ahead of the course planned on the big chart. Nothing broke or wore out and the only event worth noting was that Gerard washed his hair with sea water and regular fresh water soap. The soap coagulated from the minerals in the water and glued his long hair into a solid mass. Russ tried to help him with shampoo, but it wouldn't dissolve the gum. I thought of changing the alkalinity of the minerals to acid and suggested some diluted vinegar. I used it at home when I was in my teens before we could buy all the fancy conditioners that are available today. It worked fairly well and Gerard's hair was saved. We could now get a comb through it and his hair is in separate strands, not one mass. Gerard operated in a limited way from some kind of inborn defect. His speech was garbled, almost unintelligible at times. He was so naive that I thought he would simply die in a city in a short time if not cared for by others. However, he had great personal value from other qualities. There was a shining sweet friendliness about him, willingness to please and lack of malice or conceit that won people over, much like the character of Billy Budd, the hero of Herman Melville's last novel. You just needed to substitute the garbled speech for Billy's stuttering. Furthermore he knew himself. He had his own wisdom, this crane-legged boy. He wanted to live in the bush as a hermit, eat ducks and fish. "I can live for nothing there. I'll have some sheep and make my own boots out of sheepskin. I don't like cities and fancy things." He talked on and on about how he would make the boots. It was like an obsession for several days and then forgotten.

The day's run was 124 nautical miles.

August 6. This day passed as beautifully as the last. The same little fluffy clouds, the same light, steady winds. There was a regular pattern developing of wind dropping at night and then picking up some during the day. Even so we dropped the genny and raised the jib at sundown as a matter of caution in case of squalls. Getting the genny down in the middle of the night with an inexperienced crew could be quite dramatic, even hazardous. I was still somewhat conditioned by my experiences in the Southern Ocean. There I expected all hell to break loose at night and it usually did. Maybe I was too cautious now.

We were making a very good passage. Both our total distance traveled and our easting was better than I had hoped for. The conditions on the boat were very pleasant—not a drop of water below and very little motion. I could sail like this forever. It was just like being in a movie of the South Pacific.

Russ called my attention to the fact that the lower bobstay was a little loose. He thought that the forestay might need tightening. The upper bobstay was tight so that couldn't have been the problem. The fault seemed to be with the ring bolt at the stem. It was rusted badly and was bent up. I was afraid it could be rusted out inside the stem. There wasn't much I could do to repair it, but I wasn't going to push it too hard. The genny would come down as soon as whitecaps appeared. Thank God for the double bobstays.

The day's run was 109 nautical miles.

August 7. Today I repaired the head of the mule with a heavy lashing of marline and a hose clamp. We went to set it and discovered that Gerard had brought the halyard down on the wrong side of the spreaders when he retrieved it in Papeete. He and Harry figured out a way to take a weight aloft on the halyard and swing it over the spreaders. It worked, much to their delight, and we promptly put up the mule. It is a good sail for this point of the wind and gives us an extra half knot. It's easy to set and lower and looks great. Yes, even under these conditions aesthetics has its value. We planned to leave it up at night in good weather.

We were getting close to the equator and the sun was quite intense although it wasn't really hot on deck because of the wind. The crew still wore "oilies" at night when they were on watch, but it was warm enough below to sleep uncovered since we all slept in our clothes. The sun was still at about 16 degrees N latitude, moving south, of course. Russ and I figured that it would be directly overhead about August 14 when we would share the same latitude. I figured we should cross the equator the afternoon of the 9th. I needed to plan a ceremony. It was an old tradition all over the world in the navies and merchant marines to have an initiation ceremony for sailors who have never crossed the equator. They were called Pollywogs. The initiation rites in which they were initiated into the Kingdom of Neptune could often be a bit rough and were arranged by the sailors called Shellbacks who had previously made the crossing. One of them was designated as King Neptune and was officially chosen to lead the ceremonies. The Pollywogs were sometimes dressed up as women, or eggs were cracked on their heads. They might be forced into some kind of physical test like crawling across slippery decks on their hands and knees while being swatted with lengths of hose. The Shellbacks thought of plenty of other silly things. We were all Pollywogs on Narhval because only crossing the equator by boat counts so we would have to make some adjustments to the customs.

Late in the afternoon we backed the sails while taking down the genny. We had the jib down and I didn't think we could come about without it so I put the rudder amidships and went forward to lend a hand. The result was that we backed down on the taffrail log and the line caught on the rudder. Damn! About the fourth or fifth time this had happened. I fiddled around with it, moving it from side to side and jiggling it with care since I didn't want to break it. The day's run was 86.5 nautical miles.

August 8. We managed to get the log line and spinner loose from the rudder early in the morning, but wouldn't have a valid DR for the day.

David had an ugly infection in a cut in his arm with red streaks starting up toward his elbow. It really worried me to have something like this happen at sea. I dressed it with antibiotic salve and started him on an oral antibiotic regime as well as keeping him as quiet as possible—no watches. He seemed to enjoy the special treatment. David was an exceptionally nice person. I think back with a certain amount of amusement to my fears that because he came from the show business he would be an alcoholic or that he would refuse to work or that he would simply turn out to be a phony. It's strange that with so much going for him—good looks, athletic ability, great personality—he just hasn't really succeeded. Maybe he tried the wrong profession. He told me that he could have been an actor, but he couldn't remember his lines. He certainly was a troubled person at the time I knew him.

I wondered if some of this might be a long-term effect from the trauma he suffered as a child during the German bombing of English cities. He was caught out on the street once during an air raid and was unable to get to shelter. He became completely terrified when bombs started dropping around him. We talked some about the alternatives he might have when he gets home—how he could improve his financial security, which would give him a better life with his wife whom he seemed to love sincerely.

August 9. I was still worried about David. His temperature wasn't much above normal, but he still had red streaks running up his arm and a very swollen lymph node in his arm pit. I had a fear that the tetracycline won't work and he might be just one step away from septicemia. He was allergic to penicillin. I carefully went through the medical supplies that Steve left on the boat. They were heavy on tranquillizers, sedatives, sleeping pills and seasick remedies like you might expect would be the choice of a psychiatrist. I reviewed the recommended procedure in my small book *First Aid Afloat* and decided we were doing the right thing and should wait another day before starting injections of antibiotics. From now on, all cuts would be treated with an antibiotic salve before they got infected.

We drifted along all day in very light air before reaching the equator at 7 pm, much later than I had expected. I got Karl's inflatable doll out and dressed her in my bikini. With great ceremony, we presented her to David with a few appropriate words. Everyone was in their bunk at the time, fatigued from the day's tasks, but they still thought it was funny. Fatigue is a constant companion on an ocean crossing. I usually didn't seem to get as tired as the others. Maybe my motivation to get my boat back kept me going. The day's run was 102 nautical miles.

August 10. David was definitely better! What a relief! If I were to go to sea again I would make up my own medical kit with a doctor's advice and include some instructions for how to treat different medical problems.

Harry hurt himself! He was lying with his head against the forward hatch when the hatch cover became loosened with the motion of the boat and came down suddenly and struck his head, landing especially hard on his nose. He was bleeding like a stuck pig, but not hurt badly. David bandaged him up and he crawled under the dinghy to rest. I cautioned the crew constantly about getting hurt, but sometimes it still happened. Harry was slow in his reactions and seemed much older than his stated 48 years, but he had a wonderfully adventurous spirit. He and Russ have done some great things together. He had a kind of engineering-math mentality and spent his leisure time thinking about new inventions which he described in a notebook he had brought along. I always wondered if he was able to patent any of them and end up with a little more money in his pocket. The day's run was 106.5 nautical miles.

August 11. Wonderful wind, great speed! Basically, it seemed that Narhval was a 5-knot boat. She could have used a little more sail to keep her speed up in light winds and stronger sails and rigging that wouldn't disintegrate in heavy weather. It was foolish to push her too far at that time of the voyage. Things had already had so much wear that they just started coming apart. Thoughts of improvements kept coming to mind. Even the genny should be much heavier. Cleats and other fittings should be through bolted whenever possible. Blocks big and heavy. Giant winches. Plenty of spare everything. Wake up, Anne! You're daydreaming! Get back to reality. You still have a hell of a long way to go and you're going to do it with what you have. End of fantasy.

The day's run was 134.5 nautical miles. Damn good!

August 12. It was a most ordinary beautiful day in the middle of the Pacific Ocean with steady light to moderate southeast winds and rhythmic waves. Big puffy clouds floated with regularity across a cerulean blue sky. Sea birds flew past or dove into the sea around us. Nothing broke or went wrong. It seemed almost miraculous. The day's run was 124 nautical miles.

August 13. The day started out very differently from the last one. There was a dark sky overhead filled with many heavy clouds and frequent squalls in the midst of very light airs. Some packed quite a lot of wind and I knew I should have changed the genny for the jib, but I was so turned on over having reached the doldrums, so filled with the spirit of the sea, that I just left everything up and let Narhval move with the wind. I steered from 7:30 am to 4 pm then became bored with the calm that descended on us. I also became impatient with the crew. They had moped around the last couple of days, especially David who I know must have felt that it was taking forever to get to Hawaii. He is absolutely sick and tired of being in the middle of the ocean with all its stresses and discomforts. He has been downright sulky and defensive about everything I say to him. Now, after being becalmed only a couple of hours they were all grumbling because I didn't want to start the engine. I tried to explain that the engine wasn't running well and could quit and we needed to save it for when we really needed it, like getting into Honolulu. I swore that if I ever did anything like this again I would have a smaller boat and I would equip the boat with big winches, a pulpit, self-steering gear and I would single hand! I guess I was moping around just like I mentally accused the crew of doing, but didn't see it that way. It was cabin fever, plain and simple. All the symptoms were there.

August 14. A moderate wind came up early in the morning and we raised the sails. It was Gerard's birthday with early morning greetings from all. He was sweet 16. I baked him a chocolate cake that fell apart and looked crazy, but tasted great. Late in the day a huge school of dolphins swam by the boat over a period of several hours. There was a general discussion concerning whether they were dolphins or porpoises or whether these were alternate names for the same creatures. Since they had curved dorsal fins and were swimming in the open ocean rather than near land, I thought they were dolphins. Porpoises have triangular dorsal fins and occur closer to land. However, contrary to this rule, some species of dolphins inhabit rivers including the Ganges in India, the Yangtze in China (may be extinct) and the Amazon River of South America. I think they may be only distantly related to the marine dolphins that played around our boat that day, leaping, diving, speeding and turning triple twists in the air as they went by. We told Gerard that they had come for his birthday. I think he believed it and should have for that matter.

It was a very slow day. The sails slatted badly and I thought about starting the engine to ease some of the personal tensions, but the batteries were only half charged and I knew we'd need them for the compass light.

August 15. I got up early to a beautiful calm morning and had my coffee and the sea to myself. I had a chance just to think about how the trip had changed me, strengthened me, and had confirmed my close relations with the sea. I'd never be quite the same again. My thoughts went on like a little conversation with my husband. "I hope you feel the same way about it, Max, and we'll sail together for the rest of our lives. If I'm ever left alone I'll sail by myself until the sea just swallows me up."

At about 8 am Gerard and David presented themselves on deck as a protest committee from the fo'c'sle (fore-castle). They wanted to start the engine and were very insistent about it. They were totally out of patience after 2 days of light winds and calms. I don't think that either of them really belonged on a cruising sailboat. Gerard really liked small boat racing. Ringleader, our former race boat, would have been his perfect boat. David would have liked going to Catalina Island on a trimaran in calm weather in the summer with his wife and Hollywood friends. I didn't want to start the engine because of the battery problem and I thought we would be in the trades soon, but I know real human distress when I see it. The linkage for the throttle was frozen up and I had to disassemble it, put the frozen part in the vice that luckily was aboard and beat the hell out of it to loosen it. I installed new bolts and nuts on the fixed rocker arm. After about an hour's hot work we were able to start the engine. Russ had to take the McCulloch apart completely before he could get it to work and recharge the batteries. Everyone was happy for awhile, but about 5 pm the cooling water pump shut down and we had to turn the engine off. We put the sails up for what little wind there was. By 9 pm it was gone except for the squalls that came and went suddenly. We rolled around the rest of the night.

August 16 and 17. We had a shitty night followed by a shitty morning. It was cloudy with steady drizzle and a lumpy sea. We slatted maddeningly with the sails up, rolled unbearably with them down. David and I took sails in about 1 am and managed a few bad words for each other. His personality has steadily changed the last week under the stress of the voyage. He spends most of his off watch time lying on the deck and sleeping or pretending to sleep so we'll leave him alone. I'm sure he would give anything to get off the boat right now. I know he is miserable and I wish I could help him.

I reminded myself that I had to remove a link from each link belt and cursed whoever the son of a bitch was who lost the link belt pliers. It was just a reminder to myself, though. I managed to procrastinate for awhile longer.

David got up for his morning watch today with a smile that said "I'll try hard to get along." I would try to leave him alone and not add to his struggles. I was determined that we were going to make it. Actually, we had to as we had no other reasonable choice.

The wind came up some off our port quarter and we sailed all day. I should have fixed the belts, but I was too damn tired. The sun finally came out and the sea turned the deepest blue I have ever seen. Huge thunderheads with anvil tops and little cirrus crowns decorated the sky. Finally, at about 11 pm, the wind dropped, we were becalmed and had to lower the sails.

AN AMAZING YOUNG MAN

Russ Morton, sailing to Hawaii.

Russ and I have changed jobs. He is cook now and I'll stand his watches. He is amazingly capable, versatile, industrious, curious, and good-natured— like a young Robin Graham. I would take him anywhere as a cruising companion.

Being released from cooking gives me a great happy hour. Last night, I celebrated by myself while sitting on the little cabin wing on the port side drinking a little Cutty Sark and watching the sun set. After it had gone down I continued watching where it had been. I drank a toast to Max, and silently talked to him for awhile as we have always done aloud during our evenings together. The subject was, of course, the sea and the boat. Then, I thought of other people who had influenced me about the sea, friends like Ransom Rideout, Bob Gates and Barbara Cochran who were all avid sailors. I finished with a toast to Slokum, Dumas and Chichester, deep-ocean sailors I had read about and had been inspired by. Russ was understandably a little slow with his first dinner, which turned out to be a delicious tuna spaghetti. I was really getting into my cups a bit by the time food arrived.

We were becalmed again during the night and rose to a windless morning. I knew I had to get the engine going and get to a better latitude where we could pick up the trade winds. About 7 am with 2 screwdrivers and many curses I removed one link from each belt. We started the engine and the cooling pump worked!

August 18. We ran the engine for 21 hours and with the rising sun we were in the NE trade winds. They arrived as a squall and were almost too fierce to begin with. Later, at about 9 am, they died down to nothing and we were left with a lumpy sea.

Russ began cleaning up the galley from last night's dinner. He has taken his new job with his usual competence. Harry, his father, had a totally different personality. He was the paper and pencil idea man, the intellectual on the boat. He seemed to have very little practical interest in the boat or in sailing. So far, he hadn't learned the names or positions of any of the lines. He was so intelligent that I'm sure he could have learned them in a few minutes if he had wanted to, but I didn't think he saw it as important or interesting in any way. Since he lacked the kind of physical coordination and agility that he needed for getting around on the deck of a boat at sea I lived in constant fear he would injure himself. He seemed to have so little energy that I found myself wondering if he had a chronic health problem of some sort. I certainly hoped not because he was such a nice person he deserved the best. He was cheerful even when most of us were not, patient when the rest of us had had it up to our jugular veins and surprisingly adventurous. He was willing to live in a very simple way—eat almost anything, sleep anywhere. He had provided an outstanding environment for his three adopted children, including Russ. They had a secure, loving home with a measure each of freedom and structure.

More engine problems. The link belts have stretched more. The engine was running hot. I went down to turn off the port fuel tank and found oil spurting out the ventilator. The oil measured 0 on the dip stick. I changed the oil filter element and when we started the engine the oil stayed where it belonged.

The wind came up with a moderate force about noon and stayed steady all afternoon. We were able to fly the mule and the genny. People's spirits were up with the wind, especially David's.

August 19. We had good trade winds all day. Nothing went wrong! People bathed, washed clothes and even sunbathed. I worked on my instruction manual for Max, warning him not to make the same mistakes I had made, and slept a lot. Narhval and the sun passed each other today as far as I could tell. I was having trouble getting a good noon sight with the sun so directly overhead.

The day's run was 111 nautical miles. Our total run from New Zealand was 4495.5 nautical miles (about 5170 statute miles, one hell of a long way).

August 20. David went forward this morning and, for some unknown reason, he looked at the bowsprit. Both bobstays were loose, hanging down freely and swinging around. Without support all the stress from the pull of the jib and stay sail was on the bowsprit. If it broke the mainmast would have no support and could come down. Fortunately, there was only a light wind. I shouted "All hands on deck! Sails down!" It was quickly done. Jesus! What a scare! The ring bolts that held the stays were both sheared off. I knew the bottom ring was rusted through and had been thinking about what I might do to repair it. I just didn't expect both of them to go at the same time. I got out a piece of the heaviest cable I could find and the little swaging set. The boys worked hard, loosening the nut on the upper bolt from the inside, and pounding the bolt through the stem and out with a long punch. I then had them string the cable back inside and out again from the fittings on the bobstay through the hole and through a big shackle on the inside. They managed to loop it through and around four times. They cut off the ends and after giving them an extra loop around the shackle I fastened them together with a splice in the cable. Unfortunately, we were unable to get the bottom bolt out so we will have to go on with one crippled bobstay. I set up a line from the bobstay to the helmsman that could be tugged to test for tautness. The copper kiwi penny under the mast was supposed to help us in situations like this, but I am too much of a realist to have much faith in such ideas and remained very concerned about the situation. The day's run was 116 nautical miles.

August 21. It was somewhat squally. I almost backed the sails in the middle of the night when the wind shifted suddenly. We were now within about 4 days of sighting the big island of Hawaii. I got 4 good sun shots at about 9 am that put us close to 149 degrees W longitude. I tried to get a noon shot for latitude which I had not been sure of for several days. I had a prediction all worked out from my DR and a system for Russ to work with me. Russ was attempting to lower the mizzen because it was in our way for taking a sight and we needed to fix some slides that had come off while it was down. He discovered that one of the split backstays that went around the mizzen mast and was bolted into the aft deck was coming apart. The support for the mainmast was in immediate jeopardy! To hell with the noon sight! There was frantic activity for awhile. We linked two chains together, cut them to the proper length and shackled them into place. It isn't the job I'd like, but it seems to be the best we can do for now. We'll watch it closely.

Russ made bread for the first time today and gave everyone a slice while it was fresh and hot—and delicious. I warned him that people would eat up the whole thing if he let them. He held firm against pressure for a second slice. Strong character!

I worked out the sights Russ and I had made before noon and, feeling exhausted, went sound asleep for several hours. I woke to the news that the whale pump was out of commission. The threads in the forward handle were stripped. This had happened in the aft side already so I knew what to do. I told Gerard to find a nut to fit the bolt and to thread it on to the outside of the handle. It worked! Great engineering!

August 22. Well, guess what broke today? The pin came out of the shackle on the upper block for the mainsheet tackle and the boom went flying out to port. Russ and David ran forward and held it against the shrouds. Lucky we weren't rolling heavily. I got the main down and we shoved the boom into the gallows. The shackle pin was replaced and we should have been ready to go again, but I could see a number of seams in the sail that had chafed open. We also discovered that the slides were wearing through where they were attached to the sail. Two were gone completely and many others were ready to go. We changed the weak slides to the mizzen where they would not receive as much strain and put the good slides from the mizzen on the main. We lashed the mizzen sail to the mast in two lower positions in place of two broken slides. Repairs were made to the sail and we were soon underway again. I wondered what was next. Almost everything has broken and has been repaired so we would soon have to start over again. I kept wondering about how much damage had been done to the boat and its gear during Karl Putz' difficult trip to New Zealand. It must have been a lot. For now, I decided that we should run under reefed main and jibs to take the strain off the rigging.

I was nervous about our latitude because I had only been able to get morning sun sights for several days and they do not provide latitude. I decided to change jobs again with Russ so I could spend more of the day working on navigation. Several times I could have taken shots of the planets in the early morning if I hadn't been on watch or I could have taken an evening moon shot, but was sleeping to get ready for my night watch.

With Russ's help I grabbed three good moon sights from a brief opening in the clouds. I worked one out before it got dark and it looks like we are several degrees north of our DR. Not enough to be alarmed.

August 23. I worked out the rest of the moon sights and the morning sun sights from yesterday. It put us 200 miles due east of Hilo. I was somewhat surprised that we were so far to the east, but felt that it could be accounted for by less westerly current than predicted, less leeway and maybe a heavy hand to weather by the crew. Deduced reckoning errors are cumulative, but celestial navigation errors are not unless you made the same mistake every time you took a sight. We changed course to due west. I think that the crew will be relieved to see land. We should sight the tall peaks of Hawaii, over 13,000 feet, sometime the next day. Additional sights in the afternoon confirmed our position. I remembered some lines from a sea chanty.

Tommy's gone, what shall I do?
Hey-yay to Hilo!
Tom is gone, and I'll go too,
Tommy's gone to Hilo.
Oh, Tommy's gone for evermore,
Hey-yay to Hilo!
I'll never see my Tom no more,
Tommy's gone to Hilo.

August 24. I worked on navigation most of the time today besides making bread and a pan of chocolate fudge. I figured we were close enough to the island to catch a glimpse of it. The crew was apprehensive. I planned to head up the windward side of the island, but need to make a landfall first for the sake of morale. David had great doubts as to where we were even though I have tried to reassure him that my navigation is correct. He looked over my shoulder as I was plotting out our position on the chart and saw that we were well to the east of our goal. He went and told the rest of the crew that we were off course. No, we were not lost at sea as he feared and there were reasons for staying somewhat to the east as I had told them before. He came from a civilized background and is definitely out of his element out at sea on a rough boat like Narhval. This was a voyage of necessity for him since it was the only way to get home after running out of money in Tahiti. Calms and light winds made him despondent. He was very nervous, unable to sleep well because of the navigation lights and noises on deck. Still, he has done his best to carry out his duties under the difficult conditions we have sailed in and I couldn't have done this leg of the trip without him.

In the afternoon I figured that the island was about 70 miles away. Just before noon the taffrail log registered that we had come 5000 nautical miles from New Zealand. Late in the evening the wind died and we lowered the sails.

August 25. I got up early, before anyone else, and watched Venus rise over a calm and beautiful sea. My cabin fever was showing some symptoms again and I started thinking once more about how nice it would be to be single handing. Of course, I realized that it would be nice only in calm weather and next to impossible in any other conditions with a boat like Narhval, but fantasies don't need to include practical thoughts. I had had a wonderful sea experience, but sailing such a long distance with four men in a boat with a living space of about 225 square feet under often extremely stressful conditions had been both rewarding and, at times, a serious trial of personal relationships.

ALMOST HOME

Gerard saw one of the tall volcanic peaks of the island of Hawaii this morning at about 9:30 and so earned himself a bottle of beer and cries of joy from the rest of us. We changed course to parallel the northeast side of the islands where we would pass Maui and Molokai on our way to Kaiwi channel between Molokai Island and Oahu Island, the boat manned by a joyous crew. Although the Hawaiian Archipelago was formed by volcanic activity the only place now with active volcanoes is the island of Hawaii. It is the newest in this chain of islands that stretch from southeast to northwest. The tectonic plate beneath the ocean floor constantly moves toward the northwest and as it passes over a hot spot where volcanic magma is periodically extruded a series of islands is formed. The oldest islands are at the northwest end of the archipelago. Midway Atoll of the Battle of Midway fame is located there just outside the jurisdiction of the State of Hawaii. The hot spot is now located under the southern end of Hawaii Island. The newest activity is just south of this coast where new rock is being formed. Another nearby much older chain of islands has sunk and eroded until it only exists as high points in the sea floor known as the Emperor Seamounts.

I assured the crew that they didn't need to worry about having a volcano blow up and shower them with hot rocks. There hadn't been a bad explosion since 1790 when thousands of people were killed by a major volcanic eruption on the big island. Now, as I am writing this book over 40 years later (May, 2018), volcanic fissures have opened up on Mt. Kilauea at the southern end of the island and are spewing out lava and toxic gases. Roads have been blocked and many homes destroyed. While continuing this way for several days the crater itself has started to erupt with rocks the size of refrigerators being hurled hundreds of feet into the air and out from their source as much as 12 miles. All people in the area have been ordered to evacuate. Of course it stopped after terrifying everyone for a couple of weeks and causing much property damage, but it won't be soon forgotten.

Coming in to Hawaii.

The Hawaiian Archipelago is not only the most northern group of islands in Polynesia, it is one of the most isolated. After the islands were formed living things could only get there by being carried on the wind or by ocean currents or if they flew. They evolved there with little outside influence over long periods of time. When humans arrived they found the islands covered with many kinds of plants found nowhere else. There were also a great many species of birds endemic to these islands. The native mammals were very limited, however, since they had to fly or swim to get there. They were only several species of bats and some seals. The environmental impact of humans, the destruction by introduced animals and the competition by introduced plants has caused a great many species of plants and animals to become extinct. There are now some large historical parks, including the former leper colony on Molokai and a huge marine national monument covering about 140,000 square miles of ocean environment where the native marine animals are protected.

It was interesting to think that, after Tahiti, we were still visiting some of the same exotic places seen by Captain James Cook so very long ago. It was he who named them the Sandwich Islands after the English Earl of Sandwich. On his second visit in 1779 he got into an argument with some of the natives over a ship's boat they had stolen. They tried getting tough with the natives in an attempt to get the boat back, but the natives were more belligerent and a more effective fighting force than they had thought. Cook and four of his party were killed.

The Hawaiians were very warlike and chiefs often fought each other. In 1795 all the islands of Hawaii were united under King Kamehameha. His family line reined through a series of kings all named Kamehameha until 1893 when the last monarch was a woman named Queen Liliuokalani. She was overthrown by a group of foreigners, including some Americans who wanted to have control of the islands for their economic benefits. The royal palace can still be seen in Honolulu. In 1898 the kingdom became the Territory of Hawaii. It remained so until 1959 when it was admitted to the United States as the 50th state. There is presently a group of native Hawaiians actively working to regain sovereignty of these islands.

August 26. The weather we were having would be considered ideal on land, but at sea we needed a good wind. The light SE wind wasn't enough to hold us against a lumpy sea. The rolling and slatting seemed to go on endlessly. It is the most annoying of all possible combinations of conditions for sailing. Everyone was being pretty good natured, considering the problem, their spirits raised by the promise of a safe harbor just ahead.

Late in the afternoon Russ and I changed the oil filter and filled the crankcase. I discovered a plastic container of lube oil so we decided to start the engine. Nothing to lose and much to gain. I thought that, so far, it seemed OK. I'd leave the engine room door open so I'd know if it started to heat up.

At about 9:30 pm the engine started smoking badly from the crankcase ventilator so I turned it off. There was no wind so we had no choice but to heave to for the night.

August 27. I enjoyed having my sunrise coffee alone again and seeing Maui in the distance. A little later Harry came on deck and talked about his favorite subjects. For someone so intelligent he had surprisingly ordinary tastes. His conversation evolved around such things as garage sales, swap meets and the unusual antiques he and his wife collected like items from early Montgomery Ward and Sears Roebuck catalogs. These subjects were so far removed from my interests that it was hard for me to relate to what he was saying. My mind was on the engine, the sails and the sea, but I tried to pretend I was listening. He was such a good man and I wanted to show him that I appreciated his efforts to help sail the boat.

The radio promised us 15 to 20 knot winds today, but where were they? The sky was filled with barely moving good weather clouds and the sea was glassy. We were moving at 1 to 1.5 knots. It was hard to tell that we were moving at all unless we dumped something overboard. David was in a bad mood and wouldn't eat breakfast. He kept talking about launching the dinghy and rowing ashore. He was obviously desperate to get off the boat. I felt sorry for him, but I didn't think it would be a safe thing for him to do and I knew I would never get the dinghy back so I refused to let him go. Also I doubted that he knew how to row so he probably couldn't have done it anyway.

Russ had a minor ear infection. I had him in bed on tetracycline and Emprin. He was holding his own. Later, when he was feeling better, we worked on the engine again. I knew it was losing oil somewhere. Finally we discovered a leak in the oil pressure gauge. I disconnected it and sealed the opening and then tightened the alternator belt before starting the engine. The engine worked, but the alternator didn't. Thank Heavens for the engine!

August 28. We ran on power all night. There was a great display of stars and the moon was high in the sky as we passed the cliffs of Molokai and entered the Kaiwi Channel. Honolulu, our goal, lay ahead at sunrise. Our landfall at Tahiti was also at sunrise, but what a different experience this was from that entry into a temporary refuge after a stormy and difficult passage with thousands of miles yet to go! This time it was the end of a peaceful and beautiful trip with the rewards of home and loved ones coming soon.

I'm not sure how I actually felt as we rounded the famous landmark of Diamond Head. My thoughts were many. First of all I was immensely relieved that the danger of the trip was over. Even though I was still on the ocean I felt completely safe for the first time since we left Tahiti. I don't mean to give the impression that I had been a fearful sailor, but there was always that subconscious awareness that something could go seriously wrong. Suppose there had been another rigging failure and one of the masts had broken off at the deck? What if the leaking had become even worse and the pump had failed completely? There would be no way of getting help in the middle of the ocean. Those things wouldn't matter now so close to shore. I was joyous about getting my boat back and about knowing I would soon see my beloved husband, Max. It was a kind of bursting joy that made me want to shout or do cartwheels on the deck. Finally, I was damn well proud of the achievement, an emotion I properly kept to myself, but that gave me a nice, warm feeling. Along with all this happiness there were some feelings of regret that I had sailed into one of the most desirable tourist destinations in the world and would have to leave it without seeing any of it except in passing. Maybe Max and I would come back someday.

The log reading showed that we had sailed 5274 nautical miles (6065 statute miles) from New Zealand. Of course, this instrument showed the distance traveled through the water, not over the land. The distance over the land (ocean floor) would have been somewhat different if our movement had been influenced by ocean currents.

My brief daily journal that I kept on the backs of the navigation pages ended here. My memory is rather hazy about what happened after we sailed into Honolulu Bay. The Hawaii Yacht Club kindly provided us with a guest slip at one of their docks that was wonderfully convenient and civilized after being so long at sea. I called Max immediately to tell him that we had made it all the way. He was much relieved and said he would be there in about a week. Harry took Russ to a doctor to have his ear infection treated. I had to tell my crew that, except for Gerard who was coming home with me, they would have to leave the boat so I could get it ready for Max and his crew. I knew he would be there soon. I would have to leave almost immediately to get back in time for my new classes at the college to begin. I thanked my crew profusely and told them goodbye. It seemed like an insignificant ending for such a momentous experience. I should have had a cannon to fire off or rockets to shoot in the air. Just before I left, Wayne Watson, one of Max's crew members arrived. I was glad because I would be able to put him in charge of the boat when I left. I didn't want to just go off and leave it unattended. I was able to fly home several days before Max left for Hawaii so we had a short, but joyous reunion. I saw him off with many instructions based on experiences from my part of the trip and fervent wishes for a good trip with fair winds and no mishaps.

THE REST OF THE ACCOUNT

From notes in Narhval's log written by Max on his part of the trip from New Zealand to San Diego.

I have also added two short accounts written by Don Becker long after the voyage was over. I think they greatly contribute to an understanding of what life at sea on a small sailboat was like.

September 10. All hands were happy to sail this beautiful morning. We set sails just out of Ala Wai and picked up a beam wind, but we were soon headed. We tacked back and forth in the Kaiwi Channel and finally passed the Makapuu light at 3:20 pm. It has the largest lens of any US lighthouse and marks the most easterly point of land on Oahu. All the crew are feeling a little queasy, but except for Phil, they aren't really sick. The weather is beautiful with a clear sky and some clouds. We have to point into the wind some, but are able to steer north just like the sailing directions say to do. I imagine that we will be on the wind for 8 to 10 days at least in order to pick up the westerly winds and sail home with the wind at our backs. The boat is self-steering at 0 degrees, with the helm tied down and the genny, main and mule up. She steered herself all night with a wind of about 12 knots. The bilge pump stopped at midnight and we got it fixed in spite of our seasickness. It was a great start.

September 11. We were up at daybreak and changed the genny for the jib because of what appeared to be a squall developing, but later it seemed unnecessary as the wind stayed mild. We are making our northing under excellent conditions and have logged 65 nautical miles from 3 pm yesterday. I hope to try celestial navigation tomorrow when my seasickness wears off. The boat leaks badly and Phil is much worried about it. He is a serious young man and very intelligent. Skip made coffee. I miss Anne Belovich.

A sonic boom at 8:30 am scared the shit out of all of us. Skip and I are going to try to make egg sandwiches for lunch.

September 12. We had pancakes for breakfast. The airs are very light. Our total run from Makapuu light is 168 nautical miles. The crew is in good spirits except for Phil who is still seasick. We had light airs all afternoon.

Phil.

September 13. This will be a poop day as the wind died last night about 2 am and we are still becalmed. We are having real trouble with Phil who has been seasick ever since we left and now wants to return to Hawaii. That would mean sailing more than an extra 300 nautical miles there and back to where we are now. Not something we want to do. Phil says he will starve because his digestive system isn't working. I will talk to the rest of the crew this morning about him. Maybe they can reassure him that he will soon feel better. Or, maybe he can just lay in his bunk the whole trip. We've been plagued by little wind and I hope for better, but I doubt if it will happen right away.

The crew talked to Phil who is convinced that he will die if he remains at sea. He says that his death will lie heavily on our hands. He is absolutely serious.

(This short remembrance written by Don Becker long after the voyage was over contributes to a picture of life at sea on a small sailboat.)

About three or four days out of Honolulu, Max said he wanted us all on deck for a discussion. Once we were together, Max explained that Phil had been very seasick and wanted to return to Honolulu. That didn't seem like a big deal since we could still see the islands. On the other hand, it would be three or four days back and then three or four days to return to this same spot on the ocean. That's the same as saying it took us between nine and twelve days to get to this fixed location! Very, very slow progress! Max explained that if we go back, he'd probably lose Narhval since adding eight days to the trip would make the trip too long for him. He wouldn't have enough time off from work to make the trip and couldn't afford to keep Narhval in Honolulu. Therefore, Max wanted to keep going, but was going to leave it up to the crew to decide. He said there are three of you, so there can't be a tie. However you vote as a group, that's what we'll do.

Phil spoke first. He talked about how sick he was and that he was going to die. If he died it would be on our conscience and haunt us forever. He also asserted that we, Max, Skip and I had no clue about how to get the boat all the way to San Diego. Max couldn't navigate without his glasses and Becker has never done it before, so he'll get us lost. That means we're all doomed and should return to save our lives. He voted to return.

Skip was next and basically said that he signed on to sail from Honolulu to San Diego and that's what he was going to do. Furthermore, he had faith in Max's ability to get the Narhval to San Diego. Lastly, he would not participate in a plan that would cause Max to lose Narhval. He voted to continue.

Max said, "It's up to you, Don, how do you vote?" I said we should toss Phil overboard. Problem solved. We'd have to change the watch schedule, but we could do that. At this point, Phil went below. Max looked at me for a minute without saying anything. Skip stared off toward the horizon. I smiled. Finally Max said, "Don, I'm going to take that as a vote to continue." Which we did.

(end of Don's version)

I worked on navigation all day and got a noon sight plus an LOP that was close to the DR. Both the crew and I are greatly relieved. Skippy and Don are both very supportive. There is still almost no wind. We only made 38 nautical miles from noon yesterday to noon today. Disappointing! All sails are down except for the mule which helps to dampen the motion. I've got to stop thinking so much about Anne. I'm undergoing the same experience that she was. Cruising is for people who

Don, chow time.

see the world through very similar eyes. Skippy is cheerful and hardworking and a fine man. Don is good all the way through. Phil is good in many ways, too, but too freaked on health. I could start the engine, but we really want to sail. Skip is making bread and I am doing navigation. My last fix shows us at long. 157 deg. 26 min., lat. 24 deg. 51 min.

September 14. We were becalmed all night last night and finally got underway at about 6 am. We had light air and were unable to make anything other than an easting. It wasn't much, but it was better than rolling around in one spot on the ocean. We finally got a wind change so we could make some headway to the north. It is very difficult to get up to higher latitudes, but it must be done so that we can find the westerly winds and sail home with a wind at our backs. If we turn east too soon we'll be headed the whole way. We finally got some good wind at

Skip Schmit.

about 11 am, but it still requires that we point and that cuts down on speed.

Skippy is doing most of the cooking and I do the navigating with Don's good help. Phil is still not well and isn't able to do much. He is a fine young man, but he's different. We are all under stress from nature's adversities, but it bothers him more than it does the rest of us. Narhval is not a good boat to try to make this trip on because she doesn't point well and it will take a long time to make the trip. I don't know how long since 3 knots is all she'll do into the wind.

September 15. We sailed well last night and made some progress to the north steering at 330 degrees. We'll probably have close to a 90-mile run from noon to noon. We are pointing north and working up to latitude 30 degrees where we hope to turn NE, but we may have to go higher this time of year. Wishes on my part are to have a boat easier to work—little or no steering, fewer sails and better gear so one could enjoy the sailing. The passage is great, but I find little time to enjoy it.

Day is drawing to an end and I'm going up on deck and have a little "Jack" (Jack Daniels). I'm really tired tonight. Pounding into the sea all day long on a close reach is very tiring.

September 16. We are having a beautiful morning. I stood the 6 to 8 am watch and had a solitary sunrise filled with softly colored clouds. It was all the more beautiful because I was alone and could enjoy it for its value just to me. I would hope that you, Anne, and I could have many sunrises together at sea. With a steering device we could both arise early and have coffee together as the day begins. When it ended we'd have some "Jack."

The wind has backed around and we can head north again to work up to lat. 30 deg. which for one reason or another is a sort of intermediate objective. I guess because that is the earliest we supposedly can turn to the east.

All day we had very light airs and made only a few miles. We did a number of repair jobs like oiling the chain on the wheel to ease the steering. The gooseneck on the mizzen boom broke. I'll try to fix it tomorrow. The day's run: 94 nautical miles.

September 17. We had a big night! I came up at about 2 am to find Skip at the wheel with all the sails up, including the genny and mule, and the rail down. Unknown to Skip, the boat is being pressed too hard. He hasn't had the experience to know when to shorten sail. We got the mule down right away and took the genny down in the morning at daybreak. The winds were about 30 to 35 knots. The sea is unsettled and the waves are breaking. What is really freaky is that we've had winds from around 360 degrees, right on the nose. Now they're from the SSE and we are able to head NE and make up for the distance we unavoidably made to the west the second day or so. We really haven't made good progress and I'm concerned about time. We all need to get back to work. Yesterday's calculations put us only 360 miles north of Hawaii. The crew is in a good mood and Phil has lived through his "fatal seasickness." Becker is learning navigation. I'll skip sun sights today and deduce-reckon (DR) it so I can get a little rest. We are sailing under reefed main and jib and making fair time on a course of 5 degrees. I hope to make lat. 30 deg. tomorrow afternoon and find the westerly winds. I can't wait as boat is rolling badly.

September 18. Too busy to write much. We're working sails constantly in order to make a northing. We are now at long. 54 deg. 02 min., lat. 29 deg 31 min. Getting north is really difficult, but we're still moving in that direction.

*(Another short remembrance written by Don Becker long after
the voyage was over contributes to the picture of life at sea.)*

I remember early in the voyage there were lots of days I wanted to sit on deck to read, watch the sea, sky or, especially, the Albatrosses. Those birds were amazing! You could sit for hours watching as they approach the boat, circled, landed on the water and then lifted to fly away. All that time, they'd never flap their wings. Never! I particularly like watching them take off from the water, always thinking, this time it's got to flap its wings. But no, it didn't. It would just wait for the wave to crest, spread its wings and let the wave recede and the bird was airborne, but only a few feet above the water. Now it has to flap its wings to gain altitude. But all it did was lean this way or that and next thing you knew, you were looking up as it glided over the boat into the distance, becoming a speck in the sky. I was sad when we were too far north to see any more Albatrosses.

But, sitting on the deck was a problem for lack of usable deck chairs. I can't remember if we had one or two but not enough if several of us wanted to sit on the deck or if we had a few but they were each lacking a bottom, or back or both. I do remember asking Max if there was any way to repair a chair out there. He showed me some old sails I could cut up for bottoms or backs and needles and thread which was more like twine that I could use to sew the material as needed. I used my knife to cut the material to the sizes I thought suitable. Once I started sewing, I realized my guesstimate was way off and had to return below to appropriate larger strips of sail. I did all of my sewing on deck. As you know, the deck of a 40-foot ketch lurches and staggers about depending on the wind and the water. Consequently, more than once I stitched my fingers or hand instead of the chair. Not being a sailmaker or even a deck chair maker, I had to dream up a stitch pattern to use on the fabric. Max would come over, view my work and walk away shaking his head. I told him I just wanted something in which to sit. If it didn't meet his standards, he could toss it once we reached San Diego. It took about a week of trial and error to complete my work and have a workable deck chair. Everyone sat in that chair at one time or another during the balance of the voyage.

(end of Don's account)

September 19. We are sailing close-hauled for the ninth day. There is no chance for sun shots as the sky is clouded and squally. Sails must be tended constantly as back winding results from wind shifts. We sighted a big cargo ship at 10 am. We have no VHF so we couldn't talk. It was probably Japanese so we wouldn't have been able to converse with them anyway. Narhval has great motion, is very sea kindly, but the sails are hard to work because there is no mechanical gear for tending them. The sheets are all operated with block and tackle. We were becalmed with most of the sails down at 4 pm. Skippy screwed up the battery charger by starting the engine while charging. This shorts out the charger. The crew is not too happy tonight. No wind at midnight. We're hung up on this part of the ocean. Maybe we'll do better tomorrow.

September 20. The wind came up about 2 pm and was fair. It was our first day with the wind abaft the beam. It's now 1900 and the wind has held all day. Great sail! I love every puff and every gust and do not mind water over the bow or the problems associated with a hard run. We're now under reefed main and jib and making 5 knots. Phil fixed dinner and it was terrible, but the spirit of the cook and the hunger of the crew is what counts. Again, the boat is wonderful in a stiff wind, but needs gear—big winches and good things like that. Our noon deduced reckoning showed that we are reaching our possible turning point if the wind holds. Becker and I both got a little bombed tonight. He's a great friend! Our day's run was only 49 miles! Tomorrow should be better. We're having a real buster.

September 21. No notes.

September 22. We moved well most of the night. The halyards became fouled and Skip went aloft to straighten them. We can always count on him for a job like this. I fixed the mizzen and got an LOP at 9 am and then got a noon shot. Our deduced reckoning was way off. We are now at latitude 35 deg. We are heading east-northeast. I doubt that we can keep this heading as we are not yet in the westerlies. The crew all took baths when the sun came out. The water and air temperature are getting colder. There were squally winds all night and a little during the day. The crew and I are very tired so we rested as much as possible today. These latitudes are freaky. The winds are always too much or not enough. We are constantly getting caught with too much sail, but if we don't have it up we'll never get north. We've had no sights for 3 days and I suppose the deduced reckoning is getting a little wild. I'm hoping for a clear sky and sun shots tomorrow. Winds are now about abeam and are driving us at 5 knots. Last night they were at about 35 degrees and the sky was full of rain. We had a good afternoon sail and all hands had some "Jack" and bullshitted for awhile before settling down to the night. Sail changes at night really tire us. A fulltime cook would be great.

September 23. I'm too busy to write except to say we have very light wind and we have made our turn to the east! We turned at long 151 deg., lat. 36 deg. 43 min. at about 2 pm. I hope we are truly through with making our northing and can head for home. We have some 1700 miles to go and time is short so we need wind and a good course. The crew is happy. Don is a wonderful companion, stable and undaunted by hardships and discomfort. Skip is our best man in an emergency and can be a little low at other times. Phil is complex—rather rigid and has quite a bit of anxiety about things in general. I, by the way, am not authoritarian at sea and don't enjoy one-man rule.

September 24. We picked up some wind about 0500 on a beam reach from N by NW and could make good easting on a broad reach. We're hoping for fair winds all day and all night and maybe we'll make lat. 100 deg. plus by noon tomorrow, maybe even 120 degrees. Tomorrow will be my birthday. A lovelier present I couldn't ask for rather than have you with me! Rail down and you! That would be the ultimate sailing experience for me. Light airs kill Narhval, but she has great motion. She's quite a platform. The day's run 73 miles.

September 25. The wind shifted and died at 2200. We went nowhere until 0600 this morning. We are now sailing 110 degrees, but should be at 75 degrees. We'll tack at 2200 if winds do not change. The engine is locked up and we couldn't turn the flywheel. We took out the starter in hopes that was the problem. We can't figure out a way to turn the flywheel. It's raining and in general, not a good day, but the crew is OK. We believe we will get our winds, but the North

Pacific is weird. We finally got some wind at 1400. I steered 075 degrees (what we've needed) for one hour and then could only hold 110 degrees for the next. We made 9.5 miles in two hours. 110 degrees is hard on the wind. Rail down and really working! And happy birthday to me!

We got hit by a buster late in the day. We finally ended up with jib and staysail and could only head due north. It blew all day and all night. All hands were tired and wet, but in good spirits except for Skippy who worries about our not getting east. Except for a short distance we've

Wave on the starboard bow.

Nearly home, but becalmed.

been on the wind since we left. Don, Skip and Phil all believed we'd pick up the westerlies in lower latitudes. I've said from the beginning that we would have to go to at least 40 degrees and maybe more and the east wind will get us there. Days run was 37 nautical miles, mostly in the wrong direction.

Landfall.

September 26. If you get headed from the east, then go north. Keep going until the westerlies make themselves known. The crew is finally coming to believe me in this matter. Sail changes went well during the blow—winds up to 40 and 50 and the boat pitching like mad. Don caught a bad roll and went from the galley to my bunk at a velocity of about 50 knots. Skippy fell on his ass on the foredeck. Phil is very surefooted and never seems to be off balance. The day's run was 77.5 nautical miles.

September 27. All day we were sailing north with mainly an east wind and all sails up except the mule. Skippy made 13.5 miles in two hours of close reaching, our best run in one watch. From noon yesterday to noon today our run was 116 nautical miles, our best 24-hour run. Our noon latitude by deduced reckoning was 38 deg. 7 min. Tomorrow we should be in the 40's if the wind holds. The sky is clear and all looks well. I think of you always and I really want for us to make some great sails together. I also think we should be very careful in respect to what boat we take. Maintenance at sea is something to be avoided as we are constantly at work on things that don't work. Just coming about means that lines can get caught in odd places like the chain plates or the cathead. We had dinner of corned beef, mashed potatoes and beans plus Jack Daniels, my favorite dessert.

There was very little sun this morning, but I grabbed a 9 am shot and then an uncertain one around 11:30 that put us at lat. 40 deg. 19 min. and long. 144 deg. All hands are anxious to pick up westerlies and head for the east. We are now steering 40 degrees as the wind has swung more to the south. It seems that we are going to have a slow trip.

September 29. We steered east all night and well into the afternoon. Odd, but we are making our easting at a latitude over 40 degrees without the westerlies. Our wind is out of the south! If it heads us we will go north again, but I'm of the opinion that the westerlies will move in on us as we get farther east. There was no sun for celestial navigation for the day, but our deduced reckoning shows us at long. 142 deg., lat. 40 deg. 46 min. We are currently making close to 2 degrees of longitude a day so I'm hoping for a passage of 30 to 35 days.

September 30. This is the 4th day of SW winds making for perfect sailing. We are carrying only the genny and the main and have a satisfactory motion. There is lots of sun and good companionship. The navigation shows we are at 137 deg. long. 38 deg. lat. Within ten days we think we will be close to the coast. I will get a moon shot tonight and will work it up tomorrow. Many thoughts of you and I sailing together.

Ahoy.

October 1. Big day! We did 118 miles in light air. My running fix shows us at 136 deg. long. and 38 deg. lat. That puts us about 900 miles from the Channel Islands. If the wind holds we should see land in about eight or nine days. The crew is now like a small rural community with everyone helping each other. No one has gotten in anyone's hair, yet. Skippy will work on the engine tomorrow to see if he can break the compression lock so we can get into a port somewhere and call you.

The wind changed from SW at 1500 without warning and we jibed with the help of the preventer onto a port tack. We had one tack for five days of great sailing. I hope that the wind from the north will be as kind. I believe we will keep it for three or four days. The boat is making oodles of water. From the seams? God knows where from.

All hands are most interested in getting hot showers and dry clothes. Yesterday and today we were sunbathing on the foredeck. It really has been a remarkable trip. The weather has really been good—no storms except for one gale with winds of 45-50 knots. I find myself at ease and at peace with this environment. I want to spend a lot of time talking with you about boats and systems. And so to bed with thoughts of seeing you soon.

October 5. Happy Birthday to you! I'm with you in spirit and bid you all my love and a long and happy life. Now, I must settle for a quiet communion with you. One that I'm sure you'll understand.

We have been in rather bad weather for four days. Force 6 wind and rather treacherous sea. Treacherous because we must sail abeam of it in order to hold our course. We blew out the genoa in the early am. It was my fault because I should have been more alert. We were never able to get to as high a latitude as I would have liked and never really found the westerlies.

A HAPPY COINCIDENCE

Wormsleys to the rescue.

Good friends.

No records of any kind for **October 6 to 8**. Just dates. The trip ended successfully without an engine. On **October 8,** just a few miles from San Diego harbor, the Narhval crew sighted Howard and Susan Wormsley, old friends who happened to be out for a sail. Narhval was given a tow into San Diego Harbor for a joyous arrival.

The long sea passages had taken a heavy toll on the boat. Cosmetically she was a disaster. Patches of paint were missing from the hull and there were rust streaks everywhere. The varnish was pretty much down to bare wood from the deck structures like hatches and dog houses. The sails would need extensive mending and many of the sail slides would have to be replaced. These things would all be taken care of with the application of some time and much elbow grease.

Back to civilization.

Fixing the leak (or leaks) was the job that had to be tended to immediately since water was still pouring in. Beginning with the main cabin I started lifting floorboards so I could look in the bilge and try to see where the water was coming in. When I got to the fo'c'sle I discovered a hole in the hull on the port side of the keel halfway between two frames. It was less than an inch in diameter, but still big enough to let a lot of water pour into the boat over several hours. A temporary solution was simple, but immediately effective. First I bought a container of epoxy cement, the kind for use underwater. I cut a piece of wood to fit snugly between the two frames. A small piece of cloth was wadded up and jammed into the hole to slow down the water flow. The epoxy was applied to one side of the board which was then placed over the offending hole and held there with my feet as I sat on the floor and waited the 20 minutes required for the epoxy to set up. I added a few long screws, just in case. It slowed the leak dramatically, so evidently this was the main place where water was coming in. What a relief to have it back to a normal wooden boat level of leaking!

Now, have we come to the "lived happily ever after" part of the story? Taken literally, that can't happen in real life, only in fairy tales. The road of life is full of bumps and curves and occasionally there are forks in the road. I was extremely happy to have Narhval back in my life and

Skip surveying the damage.

I thought Max was pleased as well. We had several lovely trips to Catalina Island which lay about 50 nautical miles from San Diego Harbor, a long day's sail. We continued to do local sailing, but I noticed that complaints from Max about the boat were becoming more frequent and more insistent. He wanted to join the yacht club and enter into some of the local round-the-buoy type races, but Narhval was too damned slow. We couldn't even begin to compete. The slowness and the fact that Narhval looked more like a workboat than a yacht killed his spirit, as he told me over and over. I knew very well what was in store. I was being prepared for selling Narhval and buying another boat that would make Max happier.

I realized that another great ocean adventure was very unlikely so our sailing would be confined to local waters and would probably consist mostly of sailing back and forth in the bay. Why not do it in something that would make my husband happy? We said goodbye to Narhval again with great relief on Max's part and more than a little sadness on mine.

We found a lovely 40-foot sloop with the odd name of Gamin (a street urchin) and with good cruising capabilities. This boat was much more to Max's liking and one that I also appreciated. I even indulged in a few fantasies about cruising through the islands of the South Pacific. Then Gullmar came on the scene. She was a gorgeous boat, a 45-foot ocean-racing sloop with elegant lines and a tall sail plan. She belonged to our good friend Jerry Taylor. Jerry wanted to sell her and get something smaller and

Gamin.

more suitable for cruising. Max explained to me carefully that she matched his vision of the ultimate sail boat. He had to have her. Jerry was willing to take Gamin as a generous partial payment. There was no reasonable way I could say no and I have to admit that I was captivated more than a little by her beauty. The transaction was completed.

Narhval was a heavily built boat, but her regular sail plan was well balanced so she was easy to control in light or moderate weather. Gullmar was a devil to sail. She had a weather helm that was so strong that it was hard to control her going to weather. I thought of her as a beautiful princess who insisted on having her own way in all things.

Gullmar was soon sold and the money went toward purchasing a building lot on the edge of a San Diego canyon, having a beautiful house designed by an architect and getting it built by one of the best local contractors. The design was unique and truly inspired. Treated poles that were the size of telephone poles were anchored securely into the ground with huge concrete bases to provide a foundation that could not slip on the canyon's sloping sides. Heavy horizontal beams were bolted to the poles to form supports for the floor joists for

Gullmar.

the first floor and the rest of the house was framed in a conventional manner. There were three levels with decks on each level and large windows everywhere. It was almost like living out-of-doors and still comfortable because of the very mild San Diego climate. For recreation we had a day sailer of some sort for awhile that I don't remember much about.

We developed new interests and the sea never had the strong pull on our lives as it once had. I never wanted to live far away from it and was fortunate to have that wish granted. My wish to travel has also been granted, but it has been by means other than sailing. I have crossed oceans in airplanes and traveled over land by car. It doesn't sound as romantic, but infinitely more of the surface of the globe can be experienced that way. I have seen much of Mexico, China, Europe and Australia. These trips have been very rewarding, but my most treasured memory is still my grand voyage across the Pacific Ocean on Narhval. In addition to being reunited for awhile with Narhval, there was another unexpected reward. When I was alone I spent much of my time thinking about the fantastic trip I had been privileged to experience. It was of great value to me in a way that was quite separate from getting the boat back. I had learned that I was capable of accomplishing very difficult goals. I was able to face considerable hardships and even extreme danger when it was necessary to achieve those goals. Without being quite aware of it I had developed a formula for greatly improving the chances of achieving any difficult goal. It consisted of three main parts. First, don't let being a woman stop you from doing what is traditionally seen as a man's job unless you really need a constant supply of testosterone to achieve your goal. Ask yourself if the activity requires big biceps and a beard. If not, go ahead with your dreams and fight the prejudice where you find it. Look carefully for this same prejudice in yourself. It could be lurking there without you realizing it and could cause you to not believe in yourself and to restrict you from following a difficult goal. If you are a man you are not apt to encounter prejudice in life's goals because of your gender, but if you do don't let it stop you.

Next, you should try to know yourself, your talents and limitations, but be careful not to underestimate what you are capable of doing. Becoming a rocket scientist will be a difficult goal if you struggle with math, but maybe some remedial instruction in math would help you overcome the problem. I learned to navigate the old-fashioned way with a sextant even though I didn't learn my number combinations when I was a child because of constant moving and now I compute manually with difficulty. On the other hand, you might want to pick something that comes to you more naturally. A passion for a particular hobby might be an indication of a special talent that could be pursued and turned into a rewarding career.

Then, be willing to spend some time and energy preparing for what you want to do. I owe much of my success to this one. Here are some examples. Before I went to New Zealand to get Narhval I bought a book on navigation and studied it carefully. Then I bought a sextant, took navigation lessons and practiced what I had learned before starting out. I was able to find a very small group of islands in the middle of the Pacific Ocean even though I hadn't seen land since traveling almost 2500 miles from New Zealand. When my crew left the boat in Tahiti I didn't give up. I figured out a way to get another crew. I got the engine fixed, taught the new crew to sail and took off for Hawaii where I made a triumphal entry into the harbor.

After the big ocean adventure I needed something to do with my excess energy. I had some friends who competed in road races and they urged me to join them. I had always been an out-of-doors kind of person, but not athletic. I was now in my late 50's, not the usual age to take up something so intensely physical, but I decided to try road racing. Following my success formula, I drove to Mission Bay every day after work and ran on the long sidewalk that stretched for many miles along the edge of the bay. At first, I have to admit, it was more of a shamble than a run, but I steadily improved. I started doing sessions of intervals where I would run at top speed for a short distance and then at a slow speed for a few minutes to rest and then repeat the process over and over. I ended up having fun and winning many races in my class.

Running for the finish.

Several years later Max and I moved to Washington and thought about building a house on some newly purchased property. I knew how to use basic hand and power tools from my days of working on boats, but I didn't know how to put a house together. I bought three books on how to build houses, and a couple of books on wiring and plumbing a house. I read and reread them until I felt confident that I knew how to do it. I also went to the gym and worked on arm and upper body strength so I would be physically ready for the task. I was able to direct my husband through each step and together we built a beautiful little house. Later, we sold it and bought a lot with better sun exposure. We built a large, two-story traditional style house with more complicated framing. There were dormers in the roof and bay windows in the first level. I helped to frame the house and did the plumbing and wiring. I also

Anne as a builder.

directed the operation, including hiring and supervising the subcontractors. My very successful homebuilding business followed with over 20 houses being built for other people. I was able to do all of these wonderful things because I took the trouble to learn how and to prepare physically when it was necessary and I made careful plans on how to proceed. This is how you can make your dreams come true.

PHOTO CREDITS

The introductory photos and line drawings and those later ones that illustrate the birds, fish, coral and navigation tools are from my collection. The photos of my part of the trip were given to me many years ago by Harry Baldwin, Gene Truex and Russ Morton. Unfortunately they were merged as a collection without the photographer of each frame being identified. Those that illustrate the early part of the trip up to the broken mast incident and its repair include some of Harry Baldwin's photos along with some by Gene Truex. The part of the trip in which we sailed from New Zealand to Tahiti are all by Gene Truex. The journey from Tahiti to Hawaii is illustrated by Russ Morton. The photos of Max's trip from Hawaii to San Diego were probably taken by Skip Schmidt. Those that show Max and his crew after their arrival in San Diego are from unknown sources.

GLOSSARY

Backstay. A wire cable that runs from the head (top) of the mainmast to the stern of the boat and supports the mainmast.

Beating. Sailing close into the wind.

Bobstay. A cable that runs from the tip of the bowsprit to the bow close to the water line in order to counterbalance the force of the jib and the forestay.

Boom. A spar (pole) that is attached to a mast or a stay at the front end and to the lower edge of a sail along its length. Used for Mainsails, mizzen sails and stay-sails, but not for jibs.

Bowsprit. The spar that sticks out from the bow and holds the foremost lower corner of the jib in place.

Broach. The boat rolls over and swings around in a strong wind so that the rudder is out of the water and the boat is out of control. Very dangerous.

Bunk. A bed on a boat.

Cabin sole. The floor of the cabin.

Cleat. A structure made of wood or metal with a much shortened T shape usually attached to a rail or the base of a mast for the purpose of attaching a sheet, a halyard or a mooring line.

Clew. The lower corner of a sail closest to the stern where the sheet (line) attaches that is used to adjust the sail.

Genoa (Genny). A large jib that overlaps the mainmast.

Halyard. The line used to hoist a sail.

Head. A toilet and also the small cabin where it is usually enclosed for privacy.

Heave to. To stop the forward movement of a boat, usually by bringing the bow to the wind and trimming the sails so that the force of the wind is neutralized.

Jib. A sail, usually small, attached to the outer forestay at the front of the boat.

Mainsail. A large sail that is attached to the mainmast and the main boom.

Painter. A line attached to a boat's bow to use for towing.

Port. The left side of the boat when you are facing the bow.

Shackle. A small U-shaped metal device with a removable closing bar used for attaching sails, lines and other objects of various types.

Shrouds. Cables that support the mainmast from the sides.

Slides. Metal devices that hold the foremost edge of the sail to the mast. They are shaped to fit over a metal bar on the mast so they will slide up or down as the sail is raised or lowered.

Splice. A way of attaching two lines together or forming a loop in the end of a line by weaving the lines together.

Starboard. The right side of the boat when looking toward the bow.

Staysail. A small sail carried behind the jib that is attached to the inner forestay.

Tack. Turn the boat into the wind so that the sails fill on the opposite side with the boat continuing to sail upwind. Tacking back and forth allows the boat continue to progress on an upwind course.

SUGGESTED READING

Beiser, Arthur, *The Sailor's World*. New York: Random House, 1972. Expertly covers all aspects of sailing. Excellent photographs.

Blewitt, Mary, *Celestial Navigation for Yachtsmen*, 13th Edition. New York: Adlard Coles, 2017. Modern electronics has revolutionized navigation so that sailors no longer use a sextant to find their position on the globe, but there may come a time when the system quits working and you are lost at sea. This book will teach you a back-up method that could save your life.

Chiles, Webb, *A Single Wave: Stories of Storms and Survival*. New York: Sheridan House, 1999.

Chiles, Webb, *Storm Passage: Alone Around Cape Horn*. New York: Times Books, 1977.

Chiles, Webb, *Open Boat: Across the Pacific*. New York: W. W. Norton & Company, 1982. A 7,000-mile sailing trip across the Pacific in an open 18-foot yawl. One of seven books from a sailor who has made five solo circumnavigations.

Graham, Robin L. with Derek L. T. Gill, *Dove*. TBS The Book Service Ltd, 1972. The author was 16 years old when he sailed solo around the world.

Henderson, Richard, *Sea Sense*. New York: TAB Books Inc. (McGraw-Hill), 1991. Gives excellent procedures for preventing accidents and disasters at sea and what to do if they still occur. Amazon lists other very worthwhile books by the same author.

Hinman, Wendy, *Sea Trials: Around the World with Duct Tape and Bailing Wire*. Seattle: Salsa Press, 2017. An around-the-world voyage taken by a man and his wife (the author) and their two children.

Moitessier, Bernard, *A Sea Vagabond's World*. New York: Sheridan House, 1998. An unfinished book about the author's extensive knowledge of the sea, boats and sailing supplemented by his other writings collected posthumously by Véronique Lerebours Pigeonnière.

Moitessier, Bernard, *The Long Way*. New York: Adlard Coles Nautical Press, 1974. A story of the author's participation in the first Golden Globe Race, a nonstop circumnavigation sailed solo and lasting seven months. Also further adventures.

Keystone, Robb, *Sailing the Inside Passage to Alaska.* Create Space (Amazon company), 2012.

Sleight, Steve, *Sailing Essentials.* New York: DK, 2013. Covers basics of how to sail and goes on with everything you will need to know in order to sail somewhere from how to moor or anchor your boat to skills for making a passage, knowledge of weather, safety and many other topics.

Slocum, Joshua, *The Voyages of Joshua Slocum.* New York: Sheridan House, 1985. All of Slocum's books in one volume. Notes by Walter Magnes Teller.

Slocum, Joshua, *Sailing Alone Around the World.* New Jersey: Pinnacle Press, 2017. A memoir by the first man to circumnavigate the earth alone. It was a sensation when first published in 1900.

Made in the USA
Middletown, DE
20 July 2021